Understanding teaching

Beyond expertise

John Olson

Open University Press
Milton Keynes · Philadelphia

Open University Press
Celtic Court
22 Ballmoor
Buckingham
MK18 1XW

and
1900 Frost Road, Suite 101
Bristol, PA 19007, USA

First Published 1992

British Library Cataloguing in Publication Data

Olson, John
    Understanding teaching: Beyond expertise.
    – (Developing teachers and teaching)
    I. Title II. series
    371.3

    ISBN 0-335-09289-6
    ISBN 0-335-09288-8 pbk

Library of Congress Cataloging in Publication Data

Olson, John K., 1939–
        Understanding teaching : beyond expertise/John Olson.
            p. cm. – (Developing teachers and teaching)
        Includes bibliographical references (p.   ) and index.
        ISBN 0-335-09289-6. – ISBN 0-335-09288-8 (pbk.)
        1. Teaching. I. Title. II. Series.
    LB1025.3.O47 1991   91-21338
    371.1'02–dc20   CIP

Typeset by Rowland Phototypesetting Ltd,
Bury St Edmunds, Suffolk
Printed in Great Britain by St Edmundsbury Press Ltd,
Bury St Edmunds, Suffolk

Understanding teaching

Developing Teachers and Teaching

Series Editor: **Christopher Day**, Reader in Education Management and Director of Advanced Post-Graduate Courses in the School of Education, University of Nottingham.

Teachers and schools will wish not only to survive but also to flourish in a period which holds increased opportunities for self-management – albeit within centrally designed guidelines – combined with increased public and professional accountability. Each of the authors in this series provides perspectives which will both challenge and support practitioners at all levels who wish to extend their critical skills, qualities and knowledge of schools, pupils and teachers.

Current titles:

Angela Anning: *The First Years at School*
Les Bell and Chris Day (eds): *Managing the Professional Development of Teachers*
Joan Dean: *Professional Development in School*
C. T. Patrick Diamond: *Teacher Education as Transformation*
John Elliott: *Action Research for Educational Change*
John Olson: *Understanding Teaching*
John Smyth: *Teachers as Collaborative Learners*

Contents

Series editor's introduction

'Teaching is not aimed at the production of something, but at developing and exercising the virtues of the group to which student and teacher belong – it is a moral enterprise, not a technical one.' This statement made in the final chapter provide us with the essence of John Olson's thinking, and points to the unique quality of this book. Like Smyth's book in the series, it emphasizes the complexity and artistry of teaching, rejecting as trivializing and misleading attempts over the years to define it as a craft and to analyse it as a series of atomistic acts.

The book aims to contribute to the debate about better teaching and better ways for teachers to learn from their experience by offering a detailed method for critically analysing and evaluating practice through analysis of change processes. It rejects the justification and improvement of practice through quasi-scientific approaches as being false paths, arguing that excellence in teaching is primarily dependent upon the virtues of honesty, courage and justice. Like Elliott in this series, John Olson asserts that tacit knowledge precedes articulated knowledge (i.e. much teaching is based upon intuition) and that teacher development, if it is to be effective, should be aimed at enhancing the capacity to understand one's own practice. In a number of case studies presented, he criticizes those externally generated innovations which fail to seek an understanding of the deep structures of classroom practice and thus do not match visions with the teachers. He analyses, through case studies of the change process in classrooms, the importance of the rituals and routines which 'reflect judgements teachers make about how to structure daily life in their classrooms', and which help teachers resolve the dilemmas of teaching.

The book presents a close examination of change processes in action, demonstrating that change is a process of dialogue in which 'old and new practices speak to each other' through critical reflection upon practice by teachers themselves who must, by definition, know more than external 'experts' about what they do. It follows, then, that those kinds of teacher development which are thinly disguised processes of teacher manipulation should be avoided as ineffective. The critical interpretation of events in classrooms should be controlled by teachers themselves as members of a community of workers concerned to do 'worthwhile things' in schools.

Like that of Elliott and Smyth in this series, John Olson's research reveals the necessity of recognizing the centrality of teachers in their own development and in the formulation of policy which is designed to change classrooms and schools. Effective change in classrooms will not occur until it ceases to be regarded as a mere technical-rational process and unless explanations of classroom life by teachers themselves are actively sought. This book is a 'must' for all those concerned with training and supporting teachers and establishing policy who have a genuine desire to see better teaching and better schools.

Christopher Day

Preface

The search for the scientific holy grail or philosopher's stone which magically transforms experience into learning has long preoccupied educators. We should give up that obsession and go back to the drawing board, to the classroom itself. We must go as travellers to a strange place and abandon the idea of the classroom as a kind of clockwork and treat it as a much less predictable and known place.

Perhaps this is a rather roundabout way of saying that we need stories about classrooms which interpret the events there, like those of travellers who reported on events in far off places. Clifford Geertz (1973) wrote such accounts as anthropology; others wrote them as travellers' tales, but they come to the same thing – making sense of other places where we are not at all sure what the customs mean, but want to find out. Geertz's book, *The Interpretation of Cultures*, is a classic in this regard – a guide for those who want to make sense of faraway places with strange customs. Classrooms are such faraway places with strange customs, in my view.

What does it mean to write such accounts? Geertz points out that interpretation – the process involved – is a fictive process – an imaginative act of an author who makes something out of what was said and seen. He says (p. 16) that we should not think that because of this picture, or imaginative element, interpretative accounts are merely 'scholarly artifice'. He says:

> The claim to attention of an ethnographic account ... [rests] on the degree to which [the author] is able to clarify what goes on ... to reduce puzzlement.... It is not against a body of uninterpreted data ... that we must measure the cogency of our explications, but against the power of the scientific imagination to bring us into touch with the

lives of strangers. It is not worth it, as Thoreau says, to go round the
world to count the cats in Zanzibar.

(Geertz 1973: 16)

Geertz draws a close association between anthropology and literature. He
suggests that in the ethnographic account 'assorted experiences of everyday
life ... accomplish ... what could be called a paradigmatic human event'
(p. 450). Events fundamental to the human condition are often expressed in
literature:

The poet's job is not to tell you what happened but what happens: not
what did take place, but the kind of thing that always takes place. He
gives you the typical, recurring, or what Aristotle calls the universal
event. You wouldn't go to Macbeth to learn about the history of Scotland
– you go to learn what a man feels like after he has gained a kingdom
and lost his soul.

(N. Frye quoted in Geertz 1973: 450)

Likewise Paul Fussell (1980) in his book *Abroad* talks about the search for
the universal in other cultures, this time through the medium of travel
accounts. He says:

Like poems ... successful travel books effect a triumphant mediation
between different dimensions: the dimension of individual, physical
things, on the one hand, and the dimension of universal significance
on the other ... A travel book is like a poem in giving universal significance to local texture.

(Fussell 1980: 214)

Of course it is odd, even eccentric, to suggest that our research into the
nature of teaching in classrooms in schools should lead to ethnographic or
travel accounts, as if we had visited far-off and strange places. But this is just
the point I want to underscore – schools are far off and strange if we abandon
expectations based on technological norms and see with other eyes. Instead,
we should let schools test our ideas of what is normal by going to see what
goes on there, and embody that experience in our essays on the significance
of what goes on there which seek the universal in the particular.

This book tries to do just that by interpreting classroom life in a number
of settings – none of which, on the face of it, are all that strange, but all of
which end up as paradoxical and strange and a challenge to interpretation.
It is a series of essays which try to see universal significance in the particulars
of teachers' experience – a travel book of sorts – written as most travel books
are with a moral, in this case the need for better teaching and better ways
for teachers to learn from their experience. Much of the material I draw on
here has appeared in print in other places and I am grateful to editors for
permission to draw on that material. Much of it has been rewritten with the

advantage of hindsight, and all of it has been woven into what I hope is a sensible shape.

The book begins with a historical review of approaches to the study of teaching, all of which embody a quest for a science of the predictable in teaching – the quest for the magic potion which can transform experience into learning and into wisdom, and which teachers need only to swallow to do the right thing. This quest once seemed heroic – a prize to be had against all the odds, but the odds seem to have won out. The promises have not been fulfilled, but the search goes on in spite of everything – a religion based on an image of science as a calculus for control. The first chapter talks about this search for the magic potion – it is called 'In search of the expert teacher'.

In the second chapter, 'Interpreting the folkways of teaching' we examine classroom routines which are being challenged by innovation. These folkways tell us much about what teachers value in classroom life. Their interpretation helps us get beyond the surface of classroom events. We see how this is especially so when those routines are threatened by the new.

In the third chapter, 'Understanding the tacit dimension of practice' the arational quality of teaching is explored. It is hard for me even to say that. How could teaching be arational? But put it like this – teaching involves our capacities for intuition – without knowing why. Teachers have know-how which does not function like rules in the mind and is not easily accounted for: teacher knowledge is body knowledge or tacit knowledge. That hasn't been appreciated.

Without appreciating this tacit knowledge we cannot get the sense of the classrooms we visit – all is perplexity without it. It is only because we have a hyper-rational view of teaching spawned by faith in predictive forms of human sciences that we are led to be hypercritical of teachers. Teachers know what they know how to do much better than any account of it. We shall see how this is so in this chapter.

In the fourth chapter 'Tradition and the improvement of teaching' we consider how the outsider – the traveller – can learn more about the tacit dimension of practice through the teacher's eyes. Abandoning the *clockwork* image of classroom events, we see how the *poetic* might be a more apt image of the research process – the universalizing of the particular. This involves the process of interpretation, where the dialogue about what teaching routines signify becomes the basis for reflection and reform. In such a process, as we shall see, the teacher escapes from the oppression of the clockwork myth and becomes part of the reform process.

In the last chapter, 'What it takes to take teaching seriously', the universal in teaching is explored as a moral issue for the community of practitioners. We look to the virtues of teaching practice as a guide to understanding and evaluating it – as a basis for a critical study of teaching. The virtues – honesty, courage and justice – which allow teaching as a practice to exist are given a major role in the process of interpretation. Here we follow MacIntyre's (1984) historical conception of the virtues which he sees as based on a shared and evolving tradition in which good practice is its own end. This is a true quest for excellence and not just a facade behind which school systems do what the powerful in them say should be done.

Before we begin I would like to thank the teachers who invited me into the classrooms and who discussed what they were doing so that I might understand better what they were saying, what they were up against and what bedevils them. I hope these accounts are worthy of their good humour and forbearance. I would also like to thank those who have shared in this work with me – Sandra Eaton, Donna Pothaar and Klaus Henning-Hansen. Together we have tried to see the universal in the particular and it is up to you, dear reader, to judge how we made out.

Acknowledgements

I am grateful to the following publishers for permission to reprint portions of copyright material in preparing this book.

'Surviving innovation: Reflection on the pitfalls of practice', *Journal of Curriculum Studies* 21: 503–8, © 1989 Taylor and Francis Ltd. Reprinted by permission of Taylor and Francis Ltd.

'Teacher constructs and curriculum change', *Journal of Curriculum Studies* 12: 1–11, © 1980 Taylor and Francis Ltd. Reprinted by permission of Taylor and Francis Ltd.

'Constructivism and education: A productive alliance', *Interchange* 13: 70–75, © 1983 The Ontario Institute for Studies in Education. Reprinted by permission of the Ontario Institute for Studies in Education.

'The importance of ethnography for educology: Towards a thicker description of teaching', *International Journal of Educology* 3: 163–75, © 1989 Educology Research Associates. Reprinted by permission of Educology Research Associates.

'Surrealistic tendencies in educational thought', *McGill Journal of Education* 19: 66–71, © 1984 Faculty of Education, McGill University. Reprinted by permission of McGill University.

'Changing our ideas about change', *Canadian Journal of Education* 10: 294–308, © 1985 Canadian Society for the Study of Education. Reprinted by permission of The Canadian Society for the Study of Education.

'Teacher influence in the classroom: A context for understanding curriculum change', *Instructional Science* 10: 259–75, © 1981 Kluver Academic Publishers. Reprinted by permission of Kluver Academic Publishers.

'What makes teachers tick? Considering the routines of teaching?' In R. Halkes and J. Olson (eds), *Teacher Thinking: A New Perspective on Persisting*

Chapter 1 contains material which also appears in the article, 'The concept of the expert teacher and its limitations for understanding practice' in the Scandinavian journal *Nordisk Pedagogik.*

1

In search of the expert teacher

It has long been the dream of school people that a 'scientific' basis for teaching could be found. This science, based on causal laws which enable behaviour to be predicted, would guide efforts to reform the school and assure all involved that schools were doing the right thing – the *scientific* thing. Efforts to reform the school based on causal laws have taken a number of forms and we shall consider each of these in this chapter. The *systems* model used organizational theory to understand and manage change. It is concerned with the techniques of change. The *ecological* model studies the work environment of the teacher and recommends how that environment should be changed so that teachers can work effectively. The *cognitive* model concentrates on how teachers process information from their environment – it searches for schemes teachers can follow to bring about learning. In each model, predictive social science is the basis for the quest for the effective teacher. Such a quest, as we shall see, is a scientific dream – a search for a holy grail. The teacher is not part of this quest – only one object in the application of scientific laws. In this chapter we shall consider the limitations of this quest for predictable laws of human behaviour.

One of the important consequences of the curriculum movement of the past 20 years is that school systems have been subjected to endless reform efforts. In the wake of the innovations came innovation watchers: sociologists, psychologists and curricularists trying to discover more about schools in the process of change and thereby learning more about the status quo – the stable systems which form part of any complex organization. We are only beginning to realize just how complicated the status quo is. Lortie (1973) has a useful word for its complexity. He says that well-established patterns have gathered 'moss'. The moss he refers to are the traditions of schooling which

Table 1   Three scientific models of teaching

Teaching model	Origin of teacher behaviour	Role of research	Professional development
Systems model	Compliance with policy directives	Find ways of engineering compliance	Disseminate policy directives – couple elements of system
Ecological model	Controlled by nature of context	Discover causal relations between context and behaviour	Alter nature of context
Cognitive model	Based on information from environment processed according to rules	Discover how information processing is correlated to learning outcomes	Teach information processing skills

have become rituals and so inert that they have gathered moss – so Lortie suggests. But these very rituals reflect something more than inertia – they reflect wisdom, purpose and value. Why should he spurn them out of hand without knowing what they mean?

The current dominant conceptions of school change do not give proper attention to these traditions and to the role that teachers ought to play in understanding them and transforming them. The teacher is reduced to an element to be manipulated within a framework of social control based on social science theory. One consequence is that the important moral agency of the teacher is reduced to an instrument in a technical rational plan – no dialogue here. Let us see how this is so.

Three approaches to change can be commonly found guiding theory and practice; these I call systems, ecological and cognitive approaches (see Table 1). While all emphasize that external factors shape change, they have interesting differences which we look at now as we try to understand why these approaches so dominate thinking about professional development and school improvement. We begin with the systems approach.

The systems model

The systems conception might also be called the bureaucratic. The idea behind this conception is that inputs (decisions) and outputs (what happens in the classroom) can be tightly coupled (Weick 1976). Parts of the system are arranged to ensure that central directives will be implemented – people will act according to system plans and, if they don't, the nature of the system will be adjusted to improve the link between input and outputs. It is assumed that those in the system find the goals understandable and that the technical capacity exists to implement those goals.

Now much of the literature on school change reflects a systems approach. Teachers behave according to systems plans which are the basis for describing their behaviour. In one approach, the concerns of teachers are diagnosed. These are concerns that they ought to have about the innovation if they are to make 'effective' use of it. As well a Level of Use (LoU) instrument (Hall and Loucks 1977) is used to determine the extent to which the innovation has been translated into teacher behaviour defined by the design of the innovation. The aim in gathering this data is to measure implementation in a 'cost-feasible manner'. The LoU instrument is a scale against which people's responses to systems plans can be measured. As the authors say, 'The focus is not on how they feel (think) but on what they do in relation to the innovation.' That is on the extent to which they behave in conformity with the desired behaviour.

In this systems conception, practice itself is seen to require scientific control. The LoU instrument brings scientific precision to bear on the problems of managing change; assessments of teachers are used to help people accommodate to the plans of the organization.

Defining teacher behaviour in terms of system norms can be seen in the typology of teacher response to change developed by Doyle and Ponder (1977) based on the work of Sieber (1972).

Sieber identifies three types of teachers: the rational type, the co-operator type and the powerless type. The rational type, according to Sieber, bases decisions on the best available information concerning the likely outcomes of action. Such a person, he says, is best influenced by books, lectures, information. The co-operator is a person who wants to volunteer and only needs to be shown an appropriate direction in order that his commitment be secured. Such a person needs to be talked to by a consultant. The powerless functionary remains inert and must be instructed to obey. Instructions are sent and evidence of compliance required.

Sieber evaluates each change strategy, which is tailor-made according to the type of teacher, in terms of its efficiency in bringing about change. Efficiency is assessed on the basis of effort, coverage obtained and yield. He finds none of these approaches adequate in itself, and proposes a combined approach based on his analysis of what inducements in schools promote innovative behaviour. In his model external factors are manipulated to induce compliance with system plans.

Based on Sieber's work Doyle and Ponder (1977) developed a similar guide to managing the change process. The rational adopter, they say, is persuaded by 'information dissemination and deliberative mechanisms'. The stone-age obstructionist, like Sieber's powerless functionary, tends not to react to change proposals, but to continue ever onwards with a primitive technology. This type has to be either ordered to do the new thing or is bypassed by teacher-proofed materials. Most teachers are pragmatic sceptics who adhere to the 'practicality ethic'.

> The practicality ethic is manifested in the common practice of teachers of labelling certain change proposals with the term 'practical' . . . What determines practicality? In other words, what attributes of a change proposal tend to elicit the perception of practicality? . . . We have designated these criteria instrumentality, congruence and cost.
>
> (Doyle and Ponder 1977: 6)

In this perspective external factors are paramount. Get to know the teachers and give them what they want. But there are flaws in these models which render them ineffective. What are these problems?

- These models assume that an innovation is capable of eliciting adoption behaviour. However, new ideas are not such definite entities. They are shifts in orientation, new sets of unclear meanings, whose implications take time to emerge. What these meanings are we must learn from teachers who can tell us what they understand the new ideas to be and what significance they attach to them. We need to see how the intentions of teachers are connected to the problems they are trying to solve.
- These models assume that failure to successfully adopt an innovation is due to lack of adequate instructions on how to make it work. They assume that innovators and teachers construe school practice in the same way, but who says this is so?
- Teachers might construe the significance of innovation in different ways thus downplaying the fact that teachers operate well-functioning systems. The focus on adoption and implementation of innovation distracts from the existence of well-functioning routines and the need for those routines to be understood for what *they* signify about school life – about what is variable.

The theory of the systems model

Basic to the systems model is the idea that teacher behaviour is steered by exogenous, causal factors – by bureaucratic mandates. What goes on outside teachers is taken to be a cause of their behaviour. However, it is clear that these exogenous factors do not actually steer teacher behaviour in any tightly 'coupled' way.

Weick (1976), for example, sees the school as an organism whose parts are capable of sensing, adapting, surviving, maintaining identity and achieving semi-autonomy. Highly coupled systems ensure that plans made at the centre are carried out on the 'line'. But in loosely coupled systems central plans have only a modest effect on what happens in the system. How can such systems be rational, Weick asks?

One of the defining characteristics of a loosely coupled world like the school is that there is a relative lack of co-ordination, several means to the same end, causal independence, delegation of discretion, a lack of alignment between structure and function.

Weick claims that loosely coupled worlds do not provide an individual with many resources for sense-making, and with such little assistance in this task, a predominant activity of people in such systems is trying to construct social realities: teachers on the 'line' depend on those above them to define their tasks; to tell them what the organization as a whole is trying to accomplish and what is their part in the process. The purposes of autonomous individuals do not matter, only the collective purpose. Without collective purpose and the instruments to communicate and shape the achievement of that purpose, Weick contends that individuals are incapable of making sense of their work, and that teachers depend on external definitions of purpose to make sense of what they are doing: without such definitions teachers do not know what to do. He is amazed that loosely coupled systems work and he wants to find out what checks and balances, localized controls, stabilizing mechanisms, and subtle feedback loops keep the organization stabilized.

Meyer (1980), explains this apparently unexpected stability of the school in terms of an 'exoskeleton', as a system of legitimation for what the school is doing, based on external forces which bolster the efforts of the school to convince its students that what happens in school is worth taking seriously. The exoskeleton which supports the school is the system of accreditation which lies beyond its door. Thus, he says, 'the real technology of the system lies in its instructional exoskeleton, not in its organizational machinery'. Meyer answers Weick's question: What holds the school system together? His answer is the exoskeleton. Not any programme of curriculum intention, but how well the school is able to activate for its plans the support of those outside the school. He says, 'Perhaps effective teaching requires less the creating of a distinctive local world in the classroom than the activation of the larger institutional one ... It seems possible that a teacher who blandly plays the conventional role and is considered deadwood by younger innovators has found the most effective strategy.'

It doesn't matter what the teacher does as long as schools provide the credentials required by the larger society. Meyer thus explains how loose coupling works. School rhetoric is decoupled from what actually goes on. Students are to be convinced that what happens in school is relevant to their chances after school whatever actually happens. This is done by studied organizational inattention to actual work and learning. This he calls loose coupling. The key thing is that the school claims it is responsive to outside trends. The school programme is most effective in getting support if it is justified without reservation in terms of categories that have broad and solid support (like being able to get a job using high school credentials). He says, 'The advantage of loose coupling is that educational categories and instructional reality are invariably inconsistent. Teacher preferences and capacities, parent tastes, student interests operate to create gaps between what is going on and what people expect. It may be more rational to retain institutional supports by programmatic conformity to general rules combined with concealed adaptation to local realities.'

What happens in schools is exoskeletal to the classroom – it lies in the effective activation by the school of the larger social realities outside the school (the exoskeleton) that give school work educational meaning. The object of the school, he says, is to activate in the students their own membership in the educational system and with this to mobilize their commitment, and this is done by getting students to think that their school work does link up with their pursuit of desirable careers, even if it doesn't actually accomplish this. Thus statements of purpose support what goes on in school even if what actually goes on doesn't really promote those purposes. Within the exoskeleton of espoused purposes which capture support, teachers are free to do what they like.

Thus loose coupling is a way of conning people into doing their school work with the promise that this work will get them somewhere in the society. Whether or not it does do this, or ought to do this, isn't the issue. This is what to do if you want the system to be able to be funded and retain students.

Why does the systems model persist?

In the systems model, people are powerless inside a machine, pushed and pulled by forces outside of them, plastic men and women whose purpose is given by the planned outputs of the system in which they work – the orders coming down the line giving them purpose for what they do. They are puppets waiting to be told what to do. Actions are driven by the requirement of the society for the products of the schools. Rationality inheres not in the worth of the activities but in the efficient use of resources. According to the mechanical model of efficiency schools seem lax and inefficient, yet they do work in spite of their loose coupling. They appear to work, according to the mechanical model theorists, because they convince people that they work but actually they don't work, they can't work because the theory says only tightly coupled systems work – only those systems are rational.

Why are these mechanical theories of control so acceptable to school administrators? Why are these models so pervasive in educational administration? I believe school administrators need a language which is rich with images of control. It is through the use of such a language that a sense of efficacy can be projected even when it is clear that the opposite is true – educational administration is fraught with uncertainty.

Control theory meets fundamental needs for a language of efficiency.

By using language which gives his or her position an aura of specialism and of expertise, the administrator is able to convey to others that he or she is now part of the group which manages rather than is managed. It would be quite odd if the administrator did not participate in the culture grounded in technical rationality, given the difficult transition, in a field such as education, from being managed to managing.

Being able to invoke science in support of one's decision offsets some of the risks of failure since science has to carry some of the blame if things do not go well.

That the doctrine persists is also evidence of the positive regard in which it is held by all in education. Although teachers are aware that technical-rational policies of their school systems make their life difficult, they think that they themselves are the cause of those difficulties. After all, does not the doctrine guarantee a rational way of doing things? Even sceptical teachers think twice about criticizing the policies and their technical-rational base. The doctrine persists not because it is thrust upon unwilling teachers by school administrators, but because teachers can see no alternatives.

It can help us to understand the appeal of the doctrine of technical rationality if we keep this part of professional life in mind. Our reputation matters to us. That which might undermine it is a source of great anxiety to us. Working in education is a difficult place to pursue a reputation. There are many hazards in the process of educating and so little faith in the knowledge of those who practise there. Efforts at innovation often increase the hazards (Wilson 1962; Olson 1989a).

The limitations of technical rationality

Why do these models have such currency? They are based on the study of change in a scientific context – agricultural practice, as it happens. Now agriculture is a quite different domain of activity and the focus on it by organizational theorists has led them to minimize the much more complex processes of educational innovation – not to mention education's fundamentally moral character. Changing the curriculum is not like buying a new tractor or using new seeds. Granted, some agricultural changes can represent fundamental changes in life-style (Freire 1973), but the dominant process, at least in developed countries, involves a visit from the agricultural scientist bringing some new wrinkle on prevailing practice. Some changes in education are like this – significant ones are invariably much more complex (House 1974). Schon (1983) calls these applied science models 'technical rationality'. Why are they limited?

Change in education is more like a bank system going over to on-line computers. That kind of change is on the scale of some recent attempts to change schools and has the kind of cultural connotations that we can associate with educational innovation. All of the effects of going on-line are not felt overnight and some are probably hard to imagine at the time of adoption. The adoption decision is thus not one such as might be made by someone pulling a product out of a bag, reading the instructions and deciding to buy.

For many innovations the instructions are not written at the time of adoption. Focusing on decision-making by teachers at the level of 'will it work or not', as if a simple gadget were being purchased, is to trivialize the problem of adoption and implementation in education and to hide the fact that many systems are incomplete upon adoption and carry with them significant meanings that cannot be known at the time of adoption, but which are important in the long run. What I am saying is that in the sub-field of curriculum change neither adoption nor implementation are important points of theoretical or practical focus because they presuppose invalid models of change carried across the borders into education without any inspection at the border.

Rather than let the change agent define the process we have to see that an innovation is also in the eye of the beholder. What the innovator makes of the innovation simply isn't what the user will make of it, because teachers will appraise new ideas in relation to their existing goals and techniques. Theoretically and practically interesting things begin to happen when what the teacher makes of the innovation isn't well related to what the teacher is trying to accomplish for himself and for his students and a process of dialogue amongst these groups begins. We shall return to this dialogue idea later.

It should be repeated that to assume that an innovation is transparently clear to all, is to fail to see the cultural embeddedness of practice (Geertz 1973) and the difference between the cultures to which innovators and teachers usually belong. Innovations are usually produced by temporary systems which develop a life and culture of their own. The products of such systems which are outside of schools have to be translated back into school terms by teachers. What the translation looks like, and why, will concern us in later chapters.

Change proposals are shifts in orientation, new sets of unclear meanings whose implications take time to emerge. Why assume, as many systems-oriented people do, that failure to adopt an innovation successfully is due to lack of adequate knowledge for making it work? This assumes that innovators and teachers construe school practice in the same way.

By typifying teachers' reactions to innovation as lack of awareness, systems change proponents tend to ignore the fact that teachers are able to solve many difficult teaching problems every day. To assume that an innovative plan is a *fait accompli* is to fail to appreciate the slow process of practically working out the implications of new visions of schooling. The systems approach underestimates the problems inherent in this process and over-estimates the time capacities of change agents and documents to convey unambiguous messages to teachers. The major problem is that the systems approach ignores why present practices exist, a tendency stemming from the concern in the system to link tightly the parts of the system together so that inputs might more closely control outputs. There is no room in the system for dialogue, only 'fidelity' or 'slippage'. Ecological models go some way to repairing this fault and it is to these that we now turn.

The ecological model

Our second conception of change – the ecological – takes a more sensitive approach to teaching by attending to the conditions under which teachers actually work. The ecological model is based on the idea that if properly analysed, the knowledge of the complex social/technical situation of the teacher's practice can be used to make good policies for change.

The fullest expression of this view can be found in Lortie's classic *School-teacher* (1975) and, in Dreeben's *The Nature of Teaching* (1970). The model takes the teachers' work world as special. Teachers work in special conditions. There is a low degree of volunteerism in the teacher–student relationship, there are difficulties in extracting work from immature workers and teacher endeavours are often in a group context. The social dimensions of a teacher's work are addressed, especially the problems that face teachers when dealing with large numbers of children. As Dreeben says: 'The most obvious characteristic of schools is their division into isolated classrooms each containing aggregates of pupils under the direction of one teacher. This fact itself determines much of what happens in the classroom.' (Dreeben 1970: 51)

Ecologists make much of the isolation of the teacher as a barrier to change because the performances of the teacher are not subjected to critical appraisal. So in the ecological programme for change, environmental factors which constrain teachers should be altered so that teachers can achieve their potential.

These special ecological factors can be used to explain why the status quo persists and why teachers are unaware of the problems inherent in their work. Typically, ecological programmes for research are based on the idea that: 'We must find out as much as we can about the relationship between the working conditions stressed and outcomes in the classroom' (Lortie 1975: 235). Factors like class size and its effect on teacher performance and learning outcomes are research topics of interest to ecologists who search for important factors in the teaching environment which when discovered could help teachers in their work.

In this model, linking teacher activity more closely to the plans of the system is not the point. Rather, desired practice is achieved by using objective research findings from the study of classroom ecology. Dreeben, for example, cites innovations in team teaching to show how teachers might cope with the isolation they experience and its detrimental effect on their craft. The isolation prevents them from subjecting their practice to critical scrutiny. Change the conditions of work and teacher behaviour will improve, he suggests. Lortie urges teachers to become more intellectually independent. The ethos of the occupation is tilted against pedagogical inquiry. Unfortunately, he says, teachers suffer from reflexive conservatism (which denies the significance of technical knowledge), individualism (which leads to a distrust of the concept of shared knowledge and thinks of teaching as an expression of individual personality), and presentism (which trades making current sacrifice for later gain). Lortie bases his critique on what teachers *say* they do, and his critique is much influenced by his analysis of the conditions in which they work. But what teachers say they do does not necessarily reflect actually what they are able to do. Their practice is much more complex and sophisticated than such analyses might suggest. More talking to teachers and watching their teaching for some considerable time would reveal this. Ecologists have tended not to do this. They underestimated the technical capacity of teachers by assessing teacher accounts of practice against the ecologists' own *idealizations* of practice rather than probing the practical knowledge built into what teachers know how to do (Ryle 1949). There is a difference between 'knowing that' and 'knowing how'.

Teachers have always been under pressure to demonstrate the source of their professional knowledge. Social scientists have always been critical of teachers for their lack of social science knowledge.

Teachers lacked expertise, critics said, because they could not show how their pedagogy flowed from something more reliable than common sense. That something, it was assumed, was some form of social science knowledge applied to teaching; teaching being thought of as a technical process – a technique – and so has the search for an account of expertise gone on.

In this paper I briefly trace two forms of the expertise idea: the *cognitive account* which has evolved from the research which sought causal links between teacher behaviour and student learning, the process (of teaching)/product (learning) paradigm; and the *tacit knowledge account* which rejects cognition as an aspect of expert practice. Both accounts treat teaching as a technical process. Such accounts whether they stress cognition or not cannot be the final word.

Teaching demands not only technique, but virtue in order to achieve its essentially moral ends. Saying this is to say that teaching is a praxis as well as a technique and any account of its development which places technique at the centre of the process misses its point. Yes, teachers can profit from what social sciences can tell us about human life, but the excellence lies with the dispositions teachers bring to their job as members of a moral community. Before we consider those dispositions let us look at the evolution of our thinking about expertise.

The cognitive model

The cognitive account of expertise

Let me begin with the origins of the cognitive view of teaching by considering the process-product view of teaching:

> Find a criterion of interest – one representing a good adjustment of the person to the environment (say successful sales in insurance . . .) and find predictors of that criterion of effectiveness. The relations between predictors and criteria of effectiveness can then be used to select people who fit that environment better than would a sample of individuals chosen at random, or the relations can be used to develop a curriculum for training people to work effectively in that environment.
>
> (Berliner 1989: 7)

Berliner notes that the paradigm has fallen on hard times because, as he says, it became linked to a mechanistic view of man put forth by the Skinnerian brand of behaviourism and was linked to anti-cognitive views of most behaviourists. The process-product paradigm lacks:

> a more purposive view of man as an adjusting organism . . . where cognition was already seen as a factor in that adjustment.
>
> (Berliner 1989: 7)

Berliner urges the new wave of cognitivists to incorporate their research within the process-product paradigm by identifying expert teachers using criteria of effectiveness – such as whether or not their students have relatively high gain scores on selected measures of achievement or whatever else is of interest that can be measured. As he says,

> I believe that it will be the establishment of relations between inter-active thoughts and decision-making on the one hand and criteria of effectiveness on the other that will lead to the greatest growth of knowl-edge within this field.
>
> (Berliner 1989: 12)

Analyse the thought processes of the expert and that will tell you what expertise is and thus reveal how the success is achieved. The behaviourist product-process research agenda is thus modified to accommodate the new interest in cognitive science.

So, for example, expert and novice junior high school teachers are identified by asking the principal to point out an expert teacher and assuming that first year teachers are novices (Berliner and Carter 1989). Some of the teachers pointed to by the principals are designated experts, but by what criteria it is not clear. Teachers react to written classroom situations and are asked to say what they would do in the hypothetical situation. From these data the authors drew conclusions about differences between expert and novice teachers.

Experts form group pictures of students and do not attend to individuals as novices do. Experts are more discriminating about what they remember about students. Experts are work- or productivity-oriented, novices are not. Experts reasoned more – that is they are able to state the rules which governed their behaviour.

Leinhardt (1986) conducted a similar study but with significant differences. In her study, experts in mathematics teaching are identified by more objective criteria. Teachers are identified as experts if their students have achievement scores in the top 15% of the school for at least three years in the last 5 years. Less objectively, student teachers are assumed to be novices. Teachers are asked how they would teach a mathematics lesson, and these anticipations then are analysed to see how the planning ideas are linked together.

Experts, as it turns out, have the following generic abilities: speed of action, forward directedness, accuracy, enriched representation, rich elaboration of knowledge and a high degree of structure. Novice thinking did not have these attributes. She concludes that the high scores of the students in the classes of the experts are related to the character of the cognitions of the experts.

However, experts, she says, are not aware of such cognitive skills. She says that not all of these skills are explicitly recognized by the expert, and their existence has been inferred.

Leinhardt suggests that teachers should develop these cognitive skills since, it seems, they are linked to student achievement. Expert capacity to process information leads somehow to high student gain scores. Accordingly, novices should learn to process information as experts do by attending to the character of their own cognition.

It is not at all clear, however, what warrants the claim that these teachers are in fact processing information in the way the author says they are. As she points out, the teachers can neither confirm nor deny that they are, which is odd since information processing is supposed to be a conscious process. Why else would so many cognitive science researchers use stimulated recall and thinking aloud techniques to recover conscious activity from the recent past?

Broome's (1989) research with mathematics teachers raises concerns about the link between teacher cognition and student behaviour. Many studies of cognition, he says, make no connection between the formal processes of information processing and the actual subject matter being learned. Information processing is a purely formal process, but what about the role of the subject in teacher cognitions.

Mathematics teachers did not actually do what they said they did. Judging from what they said, teachers were expected to attend to individual differences in student ability to learn mathematics. But they could not recall actually paying attention to such differences during teaching. Why, Broome asks, do teachers not attend to differences in how students learn mathematics? According to the information processing theory this is exactly the kind of information teachers are supposed to be processing.

Broome suggests that teachers attend to the 'collective student' in their thinking about the effects of their teaching as they teach. Teachers refer to the collective student instead of to individual learners when they think about how students are coping with learning mathematics.

Broome's work poses a serious challenge to the information processing account of expertise. What teachers actually attend to does not have the character that the cognitive scientists say it has. Teachers say they do take account of individual differences when they teach, but they can't recall actually thinking about that when they teach. Perhaps they do take differences into account but they don't do it consciously. Perhaps the cognitive account itself is insufficient?

Shulman (1987), like Broome, is concerned about how subject matter knowledge features in teacher cognition. He thinks that teacher cognition can be linked with student achievement, and that the secret of teacher success can be found in the nature of cognitive processes. His research thus sustains Berliner's desire to base teacher development on the results of process-product research.

In a recent study (Gundmundsdottir and Shulman 1989), an expert teacher with thirty years' experience identified by the principal is compared to a novice student teacher. Both teachers are observed teaching (as opposed to being asked to talk about teaching) and inferences are made about their pedagogical content knowledge (Shulman 1987). Such knowledge enables teachers to transform content knowledge in order to make it teachable. Experts have the capacity to make such transformations; that is, they have the cognitive skills to process one kind of knowledge into another. The claims of the study, surprisingly, are rather formal and subject matter free. The authors claim that Harry, the expert, is able to select methods appropriate to content and able to see how the pieces of his lesson fitted together. He appears to have certain cognitive capacities which lead to his superior teaching and to student achievement. Thus cognition and achievement are linked with little reference to the subject matter itself.

The theory of the cognitive account

The theory behind these cognitive studies is that teachers consciously follow rules for processing the information taken in from the teaching environment. This information is processed according to steps determined by rules. This process goes on at the same time action goes on – thought and action are linked. The research claims to reveal certain features of cognition which are important in successful teaching and learning. Such features are revealed to us as inferences made from comparing novices and experts. By comparing the two we can see what experts have that novices do not.

In the process of recovering the cognitions associated with teaching, teachers are asked to recall what they were thinking while acting, and to talk aloud as they are thinking and acting. The strong assumption of the theory is that expert behaviour is thinking behaviour – that is it is mental, rational, conscious information processing behaviour which goes on according to certain rules during teaching. The theory assumes that the teaching situation is seen as a set of elements. How these elements are processed mentally affects the quality of the consequent action. In this way mental activity becomes linked with teaching behaviour and the subsequent production of learning outcomes. It is a model whose aim is the efficient achievement of measurable outcomes. Research on this process is used as a basis for developing teaching technique.

However, there are problems in the research which we have already noted. It is not clear why certain teachers are identified as experts. Is it enough that principals say they are, or that the teacher has students who have certain kinds of achievement scores? Why use those scores, or what the principal says as criteria? Such choices beg the question – who is an expert, anyway?

Furthermore, it is not clear what warrants claims about the nature of the expert's expertise. Let us accept that we have some agreeable basis for selecting experts and novices, how then are we to know which of the many attributes and skills that differentiate them are instrumental in bringing about efficient teaching and learning? Why pick this aspect rather than that?

The differentiation of experts and novices and the selection of instrumental differences appears to be a purely arbitrary process. On the face of it, the research programme and its related technologies seem without rational foundation.

Then there are the anomalies in the research data themselves. Teachers testify that they don't consciously process information according to the model – that they do process it has to be 'inferred'. Or they can't recall actually attending to their students in ways they say they do. Teachers are said to have the capacity to transform subject content into pedagogical content, but the way they are said to do this makes no reference to the nature of the content itself.

Perhaps none of this is surprising if we consider that these teachers actually are not being asked to tell us what their expertise is, but rather that they are being *evaluated*. Do they measure up to expert information processing standards? Let us pursue this idea further.

If we think of cognitive science as applied to teaching as a normative theory which sets up a priori standards of excellent performance, we can see how this theory could be used to assess teachers. Teachers who attend to classrooms in ways called for by this pedagogical theory then would be judged to be experts. Experts are those teachers who pass the test. Why should teachers pass such a test? The reason is that the pedagogical theory has the weight of cognitive science behind it. What makes cognitive science weighty is that it promises to show us effective techniques for linking teacher mental behaviour with achievement. Teachers who think effectively can ensure that their students achieve well. Accordingly, we ought to be training teachers to behave – mentally, that is – according to the norms of the theory.

Where do these norms come from? Supposedly they come from studying expert teachers. But this can't be so, for the argument is circular. More likely these norms come from cognitive science itself which tells us what effective thought processes are like, based on laboratory-like experimentation. These insights are then used to train teachers to think accordingly. The behaviourist agenda in education lives on in the continuing pursuit for technical perfection. The story is not much changed by moving it out of behaviourism and into cognitivism – it is still a quest for technical rationality and, some would say, a form of scientism.

Extending the cognitive account

Schon (1983) is critical of technical rationality. The technical account says, 'Give us the job and we will get results. We don't care what you ask us to do, we just do it.' But how can you detach technique from questions of value? Schon asks. The technical model, he says, leaves out questions about aesthetics, about quality standards, about what is worth doing. He urges a more comprehensive thinking-acting model which takes into account judgements about quality. He wants better rules, but he does not want to abandon the cognitive account of expertise. Although he is critical of technical rationality, he aims to supplant technical rationality with a more defensible rational account.

Let us examine Schon's objections to the technical-rational account of teaching. He distinguishes between 'problem setting' and 'problem solving' and has two quite different accounts of action for each. Problem setting cannot be guided by rules. It is, as Jordell (1987) points out, 'An artistically oriented process which they have often learned not as a part of professionality which focuses on scientific knowledge' (Jordell 1987: 148). Scientific rules do not point the way to seeing problems in complex situations, and Schon calls for understanding of the epistemology and its rationality which some practitioners do bring to situations of uncertainty, uniqueness and value conflict.

He goes on to elaborate a model for this kind of professional thinking which he calls *reflection in action*. This reflective process is characterized by high-speed thinking and attends to many factors in the situation including norms, strategies, feelings for the situation, role, and how the problem is framed.

Schon says musicians play music and they think about playing music at the same time. Two different activities are going on – one affecting the other. However, he suggests that thinking may not work through the medium of words: 'More likely [musicians] reflect through a "feel for the music" ' (Schon 1983: 56). This thinking process has an editorial function, apparently: '[The person] reflects on the tacit norms of appreciation which underlie a judgement, or on the strategies and theories implicit in a pattern of behaviour' (Schon 1983: 62).

This reflection-in-action appears mainly to be a cognitive process which legitimates the action because the rationality of the action lies in the concurrent thinking that goes on in conjunction with it. If I read Schon right, this account is very similar to those offered by cognitive scientists. While much of what he says about reflection has to do with reflecting *on* professional action, elements of his account of action itself (reflection-in-action) have strong similarities with the cognitive account of expertise we considered above. He does suggest that words are not the way situations are apprehended – his account of how jazz works, for example, seems quite close to the non-cognitive account of expertise that the Dreyfuses give which we will consider in a moment. Thus Schon appears to straddle both accounts, but emphasizes the cognitive elements. He suggests that some conscious mental process is going on as expert action is occurring. Presumably this thinking process could be recovered using the techniques of the cognitive scientists of stimulated recall and thinking aloud. Indeed, Schon uses these techniques.

Jordell (1987) points out that Schon's account of reflection-in-action may not apply to teachers because the work context is such that reflection-in-action is not possible – the action scene is too complex. Teachers do not have the opportunity to engage in thought experiments in the midst of action.

This concern can be taken a step further – why think that teachers are reflecting and exercising their professional skill as two separate parts of what they are doing? Why accord intelligence to the reflecting part only? Why not imbue the action itself with intelligence as Ryle (1949) suggests we do:

> Why are people so strongly drawn to believe, in the face of their own daily experience, that the intelligent execution of an operation must embody two processes, one of doing and another of theorizing? Part of the answer is that they are wedded to the dogma of the ghost in the machine. Since doing is often an overt muscular affair, it is written off as a merely physical process. On the assumption of the antithesis between 'physical' and 'mental', it follows that muscular doing cannot itself be a mental operation. To earn the title 'skilful', 'cunning', or 'humorous', it must therefore get it by transfer from another counterpart act occurring not 'in the machine' but 'in the ghost'; for 'skilful', 'cunning' and 'humorous' are certainly mental predicates.
>
> (Ryle 1949: 32)

Of course, there are occasions when things do not work out well, and then reflection on action occurs, but reflection itself isn't what characterizes skilful practitioners – it is the skill manifested in their actions. The actions themselves are skilful. 'Reflection' occurs as part of the skilful process, not a parallel process which gives the action its intelligence. The skilful action is itself a manifestation of a complex conversation with the situation which we can call 'reflection' if we want. Two things are not going on here, reflecting and acting, but one – 'reflective action'.

While there are problems in Schon's account, and in the cognitive account in general of reflection-in-action, there are questions about reflection *on* action itself. Carlgren (1987) points out that our actions reflect the conditions in which we work and the power these conditions have to shape our behaviour and limit our capacity to change behaviour through reflection:

> By living under certain practical conditions people acquire certain 'habitus'. Habitus are an extension of the objective conditions and function to recreate an arbitrary order conceived of as natural. Habitus are systems of dispositions that are cognitive as well as behavioral. By these dispositions it is possible to generate thoughts and actions demanded by the social situation. Habitus is in a way necessity made into a virtue.
> (Carlgren 1987: 99)

Carlgren rightly points to the social context of action; something to which neither the cognitive nor, as we shall see, the non-cognitive accounts pay attention. Professional practice occurs in an objective, interpersonal setting in which acts have conventional meanings. Thus characterizing the expertise of individuals as personal capacities leaves aside the framework in which those capacities operate. The framework of action itself is not a property of individuals – it is 'out there' as an interpersonal fact constituting the professional practice. Just how and by how much the context shapes professional behaviour is an open question. None the less, it would be odd if no amount of reflection could give rise to changed behaviour. People do stop doing things they oughtn't to do, and people do act collectively to improve community standards over time. Indeed reflection sustained by the virtues of honesty, courage and fair play is a necessity for there to be a practice at all. As MacIntyre (1984) suggests:

> In the Homeric account of the virtues – and in heroic societies more generally – the exercise of a virtue exhibits qualities which are required for sustaining a social role, and for exhibiting excellence in some well-marked area of social practice: to excel is to excel at war or in the games, as Achilles does, in sustaining a household, as Penelope does, in giving counsel in the assembly, as Nestor does, in the telling of a tale, as Homer himself does.
> (MacIntyre 1984: 187)

Reflection on action is part of being a virtuous practitioner. So, while we may doubt Schon's account of reflection-in-action, we can take much from what he says about the importance of reflection-on-action. His extension of the cognitive model to include problem setting, and his loosening of the link between thinking processes and professional outcomes, show how limited the strictly cognitive account is. Because practice situations are also complex, rules governing such situations are complex, he says. Neither rules nor situations allow for prediction of outcomes. One cannot make up sets of rules and teach them and expect certain outcomes. Learning how to be effective professionally entails much more than mere reduction of practice to 'attend to these facts in your environment and process them according to certain rules'. The process of problem formation cannot be ignored. Professionals do not just take problems as given and search for techniques to solve them, they themselves define the problem in a reflective way.

However, these extensions notwithstanding, Schon's account of reflection-in-action by the expert practitioner is not fundamentally different from the cognitive theory we considered above. It is more sophisticated, granted. It gives much greater attention to questions of value, and we shall return to that dimension of practice later. Meanwhile it is time now to consider a non-cognitive account of practice.

The non-cognitive account of expertise

Dreyfus and Dreyfus (1986) argue that expert practice cannot be described at all using a cognitive account. Neither the process-product nor Schon's extended rules model, they would argue, adequately describes expert practice. Expert practice is not rule-governed but occurs directly from perception to action, they say, without conscious reflection on cognitive information processing. Only novices engage in such practices.

In their five-stage model of skill acquisition, novice behaviour is characterized by dependence on rules while expert behaviour is not based on conscious processes – it just happens, much in the same way that driving a car skilfully happens. The environment is not decomposed into bits and processed according to rules. It would be impossible to decompose environments that are so complex – they have to be responded to in a more holistic, direct way without recourse to rules, they say. Experts have know-how. Novices do not.

Expertise is so much a part of the expert that he/she is no more aware of it than her/his body ... When things are proceeding normally experts don't solve problems and don't make decisions, they just do what normally works ... The basis of this noncognitive idea or intuition is based on patterns not decomposed into component features ... It is only in breaks in performance that decision making occurs ... The teacher's deliberative and agonizing selection amongst alternatives is an exception to everyday behaviour ... Rather we are deeply involved in a task where figure and ground fall into place according to experience ... No evidence suggests that we recognize whole situations by applying rules relating to salient elements. We call the ability to intuitively respond to patterns without decomposing them into component features holistic discrimination and association.

(Dreyfus and Dreyfus 1986: 35)

The Dreyfuses mount an extended attack on the cognitive model of rational activity which, as we have seen, has come to dominate research on teaching. They argue that expert practice is arational. Indeed, they argue that 'calculative rationality produces regression to the skill of the novice' (p. 36), if we have to stop and think about a process that otherwise flows smoothly in an unconscious way. Arational behaviour is action 'without conscious analytic decomposition and recombination' (p. 36).

The expert which the cognitive based paradigm seeks to find is thus no better than a beginner. The real expert remains unrecognized because the role direct apprehension plays in expert behaviour is beyond the purview of the cognitive model.

This is not to rule out reflection on behaviour that is normally not analysed. The Dreyfuses do not rule out what Schon would call reflection on action by experts who wish to consider the nature of their expertise. For example, one might look back at experiences which gave rise to one's intuition. One might consider whether things have changed so that routines are no longer adequate, or anticipate future states which make one wonder if the polished practices no longer serve.

This reflective process is not the same as calculative rationality. Processes are not broken down into isolated bits – rather the performance as a whole is related to its purposes and vice versa. Reflection on practice is useful, according to the Dreyfuses' model of expertise, but by itself doesn't yield expertise – only experience does that: only experience directly apprehended enables the expert to act smoothly.

How do people become expert? Here the Dreyfuses have rather less to say, except to admonish those who would break down complex behaviours into elements and ask beginners to learn those as if expert behaviour were rule governed. Such rules are only stages along the way. But how is one to get from following rules to intuitive apprehension? They do not explain how this apparently major transition occurs. Experience teaches – somehow – they say. We do not know what this 'somehow' is. They say:

[Society] must encourage its children to cultivate their intuitive capacities in order that they may achieve expertise ... and once expertise has been attained it must be recognized and valued for what it is. To

confuse the common sense wisdom and mature judgement of the
expert with . . . artificial intelligence or to value them less highly would
be a genuine stupidity.

(Dreyfus and Dreyfus 1986: 201)

So much for how to become an expert.

Personal practice and community standards

The argument so far is about how to develop experts. That is what process-
product researchers aim for; it is what the Dreyfuses want, too. Expertise is
something individuals have – it is a subjective capacity however achieved –
either through decomposition of behaviour through rules or through direct
intuition through experience. Different regimens are called for depending
on what you believe expertise is, but both aim at developing a particular kind
of behaviour – efficient behaviour – and reflection is aimed at improving that
behaviour. Both of these approaches to expertise seek a calculus for achieving
perfection – they differ only in the way they define the process of getting
there. Both pay little attention to the objective context of that behaviour: to
the conventions which govern what counts as behaviour well done.

This search for expertise – for developing subjective capacity to act – is
driven by a quest for perfection. But this strong emphasis on the training of
individual performance capacity may distort our thinking about social practices which are not games. The Dreyfuses' account of expertise has been very
much influenced by thinking about games; so have the cognitivists. Games
have been studied as complex but bounded systems which can, in principle,
be understood as systems of rules, or as systems of *gestalts*. However, practices like teaching, or nursing, are morally based institutions which are consti-
tuted by values laden with inter-subjective meanings.

To be a good teacher or a nurse is to live up to the values which constitute
the practice. While subjective capacity is at issue in thinking about practice,
so also is an understanding of the moral framework of the practice and how
that works. Attention only to the capacities of individuals may distract us from
considering that the practice itself is an enterprise of a community of
people with shared goals. Take, for example, Patricia Benner's (1984)
excellent analysis of nursing behaviour. One concern I have about her
account, however, is that expert nurses emerge looking like doctors; able,
that is by their own account, to intuitively see into complex situations of
rapid change and crises. Yet, although I speak from limited experience,
nursing seems most to be about sustained caring for people with particular
quirks and fears, whose recovery depends on someone who knows them
as well as knowing what is wrong with them. There is a danger of
over-emphasizing these technical essences in the search for perfection –

a search prompted by the quest to define the nature of the expertise of nursing. There remains the question about what is excellent nursing in the sense of virtuous practice as the heart of excellence.

The development of subjective capacity – the search for expertise – directs attention away from the collective search for an improving moral framework for practice. It is a search for individual perfection rather than a search for collective wisdom – for technique rather than praxis. Let us look at this idea in more detail.

The limits of expertise

The pursuit of expertise grounded in a scientific calculus appeals in a number of ways to those who manage complex social systems like nursing or education, or the military, for that matter. Educational managers, for example, are classroom teachers one day and managers the next. What distinguishes teachers from managers is the adoption of a scientific rhetoric – a calculus of control. The educational manager is more exposed than most to issues of value: education is a highly contested process. The rhetoric of control is a relatively safe zone from which to operate – the zone of efficiency which is what expertise itself is about. The educational manager is expected to be able to pull levers and make changes, but what levers to pull? How does the clock work? Social scientists of this stripe or that – cognitive or intuitionist – supply the manager with a clockwork universe and with directions for what levers to pull. It is in this universe that the manager finds credibility and efficacy.

MacIntyre (1984) provides us with a powerful critique of this dream of a clockwork world of human behaviour. He notes that:

> What managerial expertise requires for its vindication is a justified conception of social science as providing a stock of law-like generalizations with strong predictive power.
>
> (MacIntyre 1981: 88)

But do the social sciences have such predictive power? MacIntyre notes four sources of systematic unpredictability in human affairs which suggests that the answer is, no.

First, you cannot predict the invention of something in the future because to predict it is to invent it:

> Any invention, any discovery, which consists essentially in the elaboration of a radically new concept cannot be predicted, for a necessary part of the prediction is the present elaboration of the very concept whose discovery or invention was to take place in the future.
>
> (MacIntyre 1981: 93)

Secondly, no one can predict the action of others in the future because we cannot predict our own future, and our own future may have an impact on the futures of those whose own future we are trying to predict. We may think we know about the behaviour of other people because we think we have laws about how certain types of people behave, but we have no laws about how I might behave and I might affect the future of someone whose future I am trying to predict.

Thirdly, in trying to plot social interactions as if a game were being played it is often the case that not one game is being played but several. The existence of several games being played at the same time makes predicting the future radically complex.

Finally, trivial events influence the outcome of great events. There is no way such contingencies can be factored into making predictions. Thus a calculus of prediction is beyond our grasp.

MacIntyre says that the belief in the predictability of human events is an illusion and so is the belief in managerial expertise. The realm of managerial expertise, he says, is one:

> in which what purport to be objectively-grounded claims function in fact as expressions of arbitrary will and preference ... [The] expert's claim to status and reward is fatally undermined when we recognize that [the manager] possesses no stock of law-like generalizations ... [The] concept of managerial effectiveness is after all one more contemporary moral fiction.
>
> (MacIntyre 1981: 107)

Teaching takes place in a communal world with shared meanings. This world is held together by commitments to certain values which neophytes (or novices), have to learn. It is through belonging to the world of teaching that teachers are able to do what they do – to know how to express themselves as teachers through the routines of the classroom which have evolved over time.

But how do teachers come to know that world – to learn the 'action language' of teaching? What really enables them to understand what that world is all about – to become fluent speakers in that world, and become not experts but good teachers? How do you learn from experience to be a good practitioner?

Teaching is a moral enterprise not only defined by skill or craft in the production or the winning of things, but also by the worth of what is learned, and the manner of its learning. When we talk about a good teacher, in the sense of a morally good teacher, we think not only of the productive skill of the teacher, but of the teacher's capacity to pursue the good, to contribute to the growth of the profession in the right direction and to ensure that he or she grows as a professional. We think of the teacher, and the moral framework in which the teacher acts, which provides the teacher with the mental furniture with which to act.

Here the metaphor is not that of the production of something once and for all, but a process of growth which never stops. Beyond expertise in production is virtue – teachers are makers and teachers are doers.

It takes certain virtues in order to learn from experience how to be a better practitioner. As MacIntyre points out, a practice gets better because people are willing to take criticism (= being honest) from those whom they recognize as fit to give it, (= being fair) and are willing to act on that criticism (= being courageous). Being honest, being fair and being courageous are virtues. Because of such virtues it becomes possible to learn from experience to do well.

Learning to act in the moral framework of practice depends on virtuous practice. The routines of teaching show us what teachers value. They show us what has been learned by teachers. In the routines of teaching the know-how of teachers is expressed. As we said, it takes a particular openness to experience to learn one's way around – it takes a certain attitude to the world in which one is trying to become an effective participant – to become fluent and to know one's way around. It takes virtue. Being anxious about one's practice makes it difficult to learn from experience. This is a fundamental pitfall in the way of professional development.

It may seem odd to say that anxiety is a problem for professional development, but people would do many things they ought to do were they not anxious about the hazards of taking risks. What are the risks teachers face? It is out of anxiety about reputation most of all that people resist the insights that could free them from the fantasies they have about how they ought to conduct themselves, and about the real nature of the difficulties that face them. These anxieties, I believe, are related to the hazards that threaten careers in education. Until those anxieties are confronted, the search for a clockwork model of practice will continue to hold education in its thrall.

In the clockwork universe we have been discussing, rationality involves finding efficient means for achieving non-problematic ends. The cognitive and intuitionist models we have considered have little to say about how ends are decided and assume that ends and means can be treated apart. But, as Schon has reminded us, do we want to leave the setting of ends to school bureaucracies, the formulation of means to a supposed science of teaching or the induction of teachers to coaching by peers? Where does this view leave the development of the practice of teaching itself? How is the understanding of the moral framework of teaching to develop? How is the framework to improve? Teachers collectively have to consider just what it means to be a teacher and constantly to assess whether current practices reflect those values. This is a collective process in which some who are wisest will lead others who aspire to such wisdom. The point isn't to win the game, it is to know whether or not the game is worth playing.

The search for technique distracts our attention away from the social basis of practice – away from the habits or routines which grow up as part of the culture of the professional group. The routines express culture – the intelligence and the values of the group – and it is these which are challenged when schools are asked to change their ways. The folkways of teaching always have had a bad press. I believe they are much misunderstood. Teacher culture as expressed in these folkways embodies more than we know about what it takes to teach well and what good teaching is. We need to look more closely at the folkways of teaching and we do some of that in the next chapter.

2

Interpreting the folkways of teaching

What if teaching is not a kind of clockwork? What if the teacher is more like an artist – one who moves by intuition based on experience; one whose moves cannot be codified and pinned down? How then shall we understand teaching? We have to look at what teachers do and work backwards from there to some account of the process: we shall have to interpret what we see to find out what teaching signifies. We will have to take teaching as a text to be made sense of – as action speaking to us. We will have to interpret the folkways of teaching, and our way in is through the familiar idea of classroom routines.

Through classroom routines teachers express themselves. To understand what is being said in classrooms it is important to know what the routines are because such routines are rituals – performances involving significant symbols. These symbols belong to the tacit dimension of practice – what is said in classroom routines that is not spoken directly. We shall see in this chapter how the culture of practice can be recovered and how the meaning of teaching acts can be interpreted and evaluated.

Classroom routine

We tend to think of routines and rituals as thoughtless or primitive – as 'folkways' (Buchman 1987). Yet how can such expressive acts be considered thoughtless if the expression of ideas is their very purpose? It is only by thinking that some *other* language – a scientific language – is more thoughtful that such a judgement can be made. But why would one want to substitute scientific language for folk expression? Is it because we think folk expression is less rational? Or is it that we think that what has accumulated through tradition lacks warrant? Our prejudice towards tradition and folkways is yet another example of what Schon (1983) called 'technical rationality'.

Geertz (1973) suggests that for visitors rituals can only be: 'aesthetically appreciated or scientifically dissected, [but] for participants, they are in addition ... models for ... believing' (pp. 113–14).

Classroom routines tell us about what people who live there believe in because they are expressive texts. Such texts help us appreciate what we see there and to make sense of it. Teachers have well-established practices for conducting life in their classrooms which allow the business of the class to be done, which says something about who the teacher is and about the significance of what is done. Routines embody meaning. They express things. Routines are more complex than we think.

We can see what routines mean to teachers most clearly when those routines are threatened. It is then that teachers often reflect on their practice in order to recover its hidden meaning; it is then that teachers are most interested in dialogue with outsiders about the meaning of classroom routines and the risks new ways of doing things bring. The advent of educational computing is an especially good example of the reflective turmoil that can accompany change. We shall use examples taken from research on computers (Olson and Eaton 1987; Olson 1988) to see how classroom routines express important values about teaching.

Computer-based learning threatens those routines. The computer is a Trojan Horse which brings threatening new possibilities. It threatens to cause routines to be reappraised. How teachers use computers and how they construe their experience cannot be properly understood without knowing the backdrop of everyday routines and what that can tell us.

Classroom routines are not what computers will replace, they are where computers must fit if they are to be useful to teachers. However, making such a fit will jostle both teachers and visionaries.

What is a classroom routine? Consider the grade 5 class we watched giving group reports of a social studies project which were part of an integrated and partially computer-based unit on 'Fire' (Olson 1988). Each group followed a careful sequence of steps and each group went through the same steps. They took turns decided in advance to give their part of the story, usually illustrated by some material pinned on a sheet of Bristol board with additional drawings added to make the illustration more colourful. Each student took the role of 'teacher' and adopted the voice and posture of teacher. The class is attentive and participates in the evaluation process with great seriousness. Good and bad points of each presentation are discussed with gravity. Everyone knows what to do. What is going on here?

This is a complex and patterned process in which students participate in a form of classroom life which allows for personal 'glory', but minimizes risk of 'loss of face'. Making 'presentations' is a routine the teacher has developed which allows for the display of knowledge and for the receiving of public regard. Classroom life is made up of such routines. It is through these routines that the ethos of the classroom is created and experienced.

In the 'class presentations' routine students act as teachers within a definite structure. There is a large degree of predictability in what the students study and how they make their presentation, allowing the teacher to know when things go wrong and to be able to put them right. The teacher thus is able to exert influence over the point and direction – the meaning – of classroom activity through using routines.

Routines reflect judgements teachers make about how to structure daily life in their classroom. They are routine only in that they recur, but they are not thoughtless or dull. Making sense of them is crucial to understanding the way teachers use resources like group work or computers in the classroom. Yet we have tended not to pay attention to teacher routines in thinking about how school practices change, except to think of them as barriers to change. Why do we view routine this negative way, we might well ask.

The computer as a Trojan Horse

Let us pursue our analysis of routines by considering cases of teachers adapting to educational computing in a research project aimed at understanding how teachers accommodate educational computing as a new subject in the primary and junior school. We talked to teachers who were experimenting with this new subject and with ways of teaching it within existing constraints of curriculum and resources. They had volunteered to do the additional work of teaching about computers and had the use of at least one Apple 2e, one green screen and a disk drive; most of these teachers have printers and colour monitors, and some have peripherals like joy sticks and Koala pads.

There is no formal curriculum for the new subject. Teachers are making it up as they go along according to their own interests, and they express the uncertainties that come with such 'unlicensed' practice. The teachers had invited an exciting but unknown technology into their classroom – a Trojan Horse!

The teachers used a strategy with the computers which we shall call the 'teach yourself' routine. Its functions show us why teachers use the 'teach yourself' routine, and their response to its difficulties tells us much about how they approach changes to life in the classroom.

The teach yourself routine

- The computer subject goes on all the time. Students go to the computer based on a rota; students are there while the teacher is teaching the rest of the class.

- Students engage in learning the subject mostly by programming the computer, but also through running assorted software.
- The teacher teaches the rest of the class and aims at minimal contact with the 'class' working at the computer.
- To ensure minimal disruption and delay, the teacher may offer whole class instruction in key computer moves or refer students to manuals, and the teacher relies on computer 'Whiz-kids' to help those who are 'stuck' and to tutor their peers. The teacher also asks students to rely on the manual to help them 'debug' their own problems.
- The teacher relies on certain students to preview software.
- The teacher chooses software and activities that require minimal teacher support. Thus Basic is favoured over Logo as a programming activity because they think there are more and more simpler steps in Basic.
- Access to the computer is part of the classroom reward structure.

Why such a routine? These computer-based routines are not new. They are an extension of the familiar routines of self-directed seat work with which teachers are quite familiar. There are many similarities with sending children to the library to do library research, using the librarian as a support rather than 'peer tutors', except that instead of using software students use reference materials. These teachers have taken a familiar strategy 'off the shelf' and have used it to support student self-directed work on the computer.

Given that normally only one machine is available, it is not surprising that teachers have chosen to 'teach' the subject in parallel with the teaching they have to do anyway, and given their idea that studying computers means doing programming, access to the machine is critical. There are, of course, other ways of conceiving of doing computers as a subject, but these teachers all chose programming, or becoming familiar with *types* of software and peripherals as their way of defining it.

We can think of reasons why it is not surprising that teachers proceeded this way. They find that some students are teaching themselves anyway, and these few students stand out in the eyes of these teachers. They are interested in computing and eager to explore software. They seem to know how to 'debug' it. Teachers see these students as part of the computer generation. Computers is a subject that is part of their culture. Doing computers, once a recess and lunchtime activity, now has a legitimate place in the classroom. The new subject is one which has come from the student culture itself. Some teachers feel they are on the outside of this new 'culture'; even the sophisticated teachers realized that some of their students could do things with the computer that they could not. It is not surprising that teachers are prepared to let students teach themselves computer skills.

Teachers are also short of time. How do you add another subject and a non-licensed one at that to an already heavy workload (Scheingold 1981)? The teachers let the students work mostly on their own, thus freeing them to teach the rest of the class what had to be taught. However, teachers often found themselves in the middle of two lessons. They were called upon to do two things at once: helping students at the computer and running the main class. The teach yourself approach did not always work well because students needed more help than the teachers had anticipated.

The programming required more support than teachers had imagined it would. Students could not handle messages like 'syntax error'. Teachers did not say 'syntax error'. What did this message mean, students asked. They were annoyed by such unspecific and negative feedback. Teachers give positive feedback which has a 'warming' effect, but the machines gave negative feedback which could not be interpreted, and was read by students as unhelpful and cool.

Computer literate peers did not tutor. They would 'debug' and move on, and the students they 'helped' were not any the wiser about why they had run into problems. Some students found that handbooks were difficult to use, and other students became bored with software they could not control, and some types of software were not that interesting as such. Logo was cited as a poor performer in the 'teach yourself' strategy by teachers. Students posed management problems that could not be quickly dealt with like other seatwork situations.

Thus teachers were not able to do two things at once without difficulty. Not being able to offer enough help led to student problems with computer activities. One student entered programming lines incorrectly, and was left for up to an hour before receiving corrective feedback by the teacher. Another student entered a poem with a particular shape but did not know how to paragraph and ended up with a print-out quite unlike what she had hoped to get. What she saw on the screen was not what was printed because she lacked control of the word processing. A student tried to produce a graphic without her coordinates which had been left at home; she guessed at the coordinates.

Teachers were aware of these problems. They could see them in the video-tapes we showed them, yet they were satisfied with their efforts at running the 'teach yourself' approach to computers as a new subject, although they were frustrated that the strategy had not worked as well as they had hoped it would.

We wanted to explore in greater depth how teachers felt about coping with computer problems and challenges to the teach yourself routine. Using the Kelly (1955) repertory grid technique (Olson 1988) we gave them a series of classroom episodes (see Table 2) and asked them to collect these episodes into groups and subsequently to tell us why they had placed these episodes together – to give us the common features of the episodes (see Table 3).

From our analysis of the way teachers talk about the effect of computer-

Table 2   What happens when you teach with computers

1   A student crashes a program and asks the teacher for help.
2   Some students are talking with a pair of students working on the computer and distracting them.
3   A student needs help on the computer and a computer-experienced student offers to help.
4   Something has gone wrong with the computer and impatient students are waiting to use it.
5   The tutorial program a student is working on gives an answer the student does not agree with. The student calls the teacher over.
6   Students are using a music program. Other students stop their work to listen.
7   As planned, two students leave the classroom to work on the computers in another part of the school.
8   Some students are asking to spend their recess at the computer.
9   One student is doing all the work on the computer while the other one watches.
10 One student does not want to work with another student at the computer.
11 A student tells the teacher she is bored with the software she is using.
12 The teacher is instructing the class but a pair of students working on the computer are very excited about what they've managed to do and want to tell the class.
13 A student doing word processing says she's shy about people seeing her work and asks for the machine to be moved.
14 Students ask for more work to be based on the computer.
15 A pair of students have not completed their work on the computer in the allocated time. They want more time.
16 A long line of students has formed at the computer waiting their turn.
17 Students rush their seat work to get back on the computer but then get into difficulty and need the teacher's help.
18 Some students are way ahead of the rest of the class on the computer. They are asking for new work.
19 A boy tells another student to hurry up and finish at the computer. The student objects.
20 A pair of students are working very slowly through a computer program and when asked why, say they do not understand the instructions.
21 A student brings in an arcade-type game disk from home.
22 During a maths drill a student is deliberately feeding in wrong answers to see what the computer will do.
23 A student did not hand in work due at the end of a lesson but now wants to take his turn on the computer.
24 A student doing a spelling tutorial is persistently getting the answers wrong.
25 A student who misbehaved during class time is asking to use the computer during recess.

Table 3   How teachers construe computer-based training

Teacher-resolved episode	Student-resolved episode
The student is the problem.	The technology is the problem.
The problem is slowly resolved.	The problem is quickly resolved.
Existing rules apply to the problem.	New rules are needed.
A routine response is possible.	Novel responses are needed.

based learning on their classroom life we began to appreciate the problems teachers hoped to avoid in adopting the 'teach yourself' routine in the first place, and the problems caused for them by its partial breakdown into their having to do two things at once.

We could see that the 'teach yourself' routine was intended to minimize interruptions from the computer 'class', and that their views about software and machinery were based on their desire for speedy resolution of classroom problems using existing routines. Indeed, for these teachers it was not complex software that gave rise to difficulty in the computer routines, it was the complex way students responded to the routine. The teachers did not want to have to invent new procedures for teaching. They hoped that the existing procedures would work.

Ironically, their idea that programming was how you did computers as a subject led to the problems they experienced. The level of support demanded by programming went well beyond what they were used to giving in other 'teach yourself' situations, and although they thought that the peer tutoring would sustain the routine, peers did not tutor each other: computer literate students helped 'debug' situations where they could, when they could, and the teacher had to be called in often as well.

We can see now how these teachers have 'installed' the computer subject in their classrooms. The teacher reaction to newness might be put this way. The subject is taught using a well-tried approach: the 'teach yourself' strategy. The unforeseen problems of the new subject (for example, negative feedback of an imprecise kind) means that well-tried methods do not work well. The new computer subject becomes 'domesticated' in the classroom. Existing routines are used to 'tame' it.

Why do teachers hang on to these routines? What have they invested in them? Let us consider the case of Mr Coulomb – a teacher experimenting with computer-based learning. What is at stake for him in experimenting with computers in his classroom?

Case Study 1: Mr Coulomb and the new machine

Mr Coulomb teaches at an elementary school in an outlying district near a small city. He is an experienced teacher interested in computers and especially Logo. He used a software program we were field testing with his Grade 7 (age 12) class for three weeks and at the end of that time we asked him to construe his classroom experience with computers using the grid techniques we discussed earlier. We asked Mr Coulomb to group together, according to perceived common aspects, the set of twenty-five classroom events involving the computer (see Table 2).

We asked him to tell us more about what he saw as common in the groupings he made. We then discussed those common features. As we shall see, his influence as a teacher is challenged.

New technologies

Q How do you feel when a student offers the class computer expertise? How do you see your role while he's in the classroom?

A Where the problem comes is that he's going to be doing things on that machine that I may not know how to do. I have to leave him on his own as far as the technical [aspect] is concerned. I have to watch it myself, manage it, and handle the situation, I think I'm going to have to learn some of that. That's the other side of the coin. I may be learning from the youngsters. Which is fine by me. It doesn't bother me at all. I don't feel threatened by it. It's just new. It's something new, the computer is new, and what you can do with it is new. The fact of having students who know far more about it because they have their own machine is a new element. It's not under existing procedures, because you're dealing with something that's new.

Q In what ways is the [student coming to your room] using the computer to advantage?

A If you have someone there who can utilize it, and do more with it, an experienced person who knows something about it, then I'm utilizing what that machine can do. If I say no to him, you can't do that, then I am not using that machine to its fullest capability. If that information can come from a student, great! More power to [him/her].

Q [What about] the teacher removing a stuck disk from the disk drive?

A Yes. That is the same as the film projector breaking in the middle of the lesson. It's something you fix. If you can fix it, you go on. If you can't, you stop, and go on with something else. It's more like a mechanical breakdown or something like any piece of audio-visual equipment I would use. I didn't see it as a very important item myself.

Q You didn't relate it at all to classroom management or formal teaching. Does it call for particular procedures to be set up so as you know what to do in those circumstances, or is it not related to this at all?

A It was just a mechanical breakdown. Normally I don't have the students running the machinery. When something breaks, I say 'O.K. We'll try to fix it', and if we can't, I say, 'O.K. guys we just have to leave it.'

What is tacit in Mr Coulomb's relationship to the computer? It has to do with the ambiguous character of computers. Are they just machines or do they 'teach'? Are they competition?

Mr Coulomb has found that some of his students know more than he does about computers, but what the students are able to contribute isn't clear to him. However, since it is important for him to maintain his influence as a teacher, how to cope with computer literate students is problematic. While he wants the computer to be used to its maximum capability, he does not know what its capabilities are – they have something to do with the machine itself. Mr Coulomb faces a technology whose possibilities are unknown. How to exploit those possibilities isn't clear. How much will he need to know about computers, and what is it that he must know?

Mr Coulomb is concerned about his ability to use the equipment. The stuck diskette is like a broken film projector – 'down' in the same way – and to be handled the same way. If it could be fixed quickly then it would be; otherwise abandon the plan and go on with something else. The 'down' computer is like a broken machine or a lost book. He does not focus on the interaction between child and machine. What the program on the machine is doing isn't his concern. That isn't what is 'down'. It is the machine itself that is broken. He sees the program not as 'teacher', but as an activity dependent on him in the same way a film he shows is.

Were the program seen as 'teacher', then the stuck diskette would have implications beyond ordinary machine malfunctions, but this does not seem to be the way Mr Coulomb views the computer. He incorporates the machine into his ideas about other classroom aids pending, perhaps, a resolution of its possibilities for teaching that are as yet unclear. He is not sure what manner of machine he is dealing with. Certainly he is not thinking in terms of 'microworlds'. The world that matters for him is his own classroom.

Mr Coulomb is concerned about instrumental matters. Can he be sure that work with the computer will have the same flow as other work he manages? How much effort will be needed to keep an eye on what is happening? Close supervision is required, and he may have to fix the machine. Being stuck, for him, means being faced with a familiar technical problem – a broken machine.

Mr Coulomb's relationship to the machine is ritualized. The machine is something to be cared for by protecting it from students. It is like a fetish. If the machine is well cared for it can work hard on behalf of the class. He, himself, has to be prepared to work the machine properly. Thus the computer is a machine like other classroom machines (film and overhead projectors). It is a tool he can use to amplify (gain instructional advantage) in his classroom. Since the computer is a machine like the others, his and his students' relationship to it are no different from their relationship with other machines. The computer joins in with the other machines as something at Mr Coulomb's disposal. He remains teacher; machine remains machine. No fantasies here about worlds beyond his classroom which can be approached through a machine.

What is tacit here is his influence in the classroom (Olson 1982). Through his influence he shows students what it is important to learn, as well as helping them learn it. He is able to do this because he knows how to diagnose learning difficulties and remedy them; his standing in the eyes of students depends on these abilities. In order to be helpful he has to construe ambiguous classroom events quickly, but learning with computers makes it more difficult to do this. In sum, there are four questions he is asking about his experience: '*What are students learning from the computer and is it useful, and where are they at when they are working with computers and how can I help?*'

His routines assume that these questions have an acceptable answer. It is these questions that are brought forward when he reflects on his experience with microcomputers, and it is from understanding how he answers these questions that he could learn more about himself and his practice – more about the ethos (the moral universe) in which he works. But to do that he would have to look beyond the surface events of his practice; he would have to look through the routines of his teaching to what they signify about his purpose as a teacher. He would have to recover the tacit knowledge inherent in those routines.

Case Study 2: Ms Manuel's new role

Using the same elements (see Table 2), we asked Ms Manuel to construe her experience with computers. She too used an elementary science simulation we developed. Like Mr Coulomb she found her influence at risk, but in different ways. In our conversations with her about how she grouped the elements of computer-based teaching we found her concerned about her role as a teacher. Using a computer challenged her tacit assumptions about what her role was. Like Mr Coulomb she too responded to the ambiguous status of the computer. Is the computer just a teaching aid, like other aids, or is it somehow a new way of thinking about teaching itself – a portent of new relationships amongst teacher, students and subject matter? In the conversation that follows we see how she responds to the ambiguity about her role.

Q The teacher asks the students to do a tutorial on the computer and the students ask to do a game. And you've suggested that students are taking advantage of the teacher. I just wondered what the type of advantage was.

A It's the one where they try to either see if they can wear you down – nag you long enough, or bug you long enough – so they can end up doing what they want.

Q Getting their way?

A Thinking that you don't either have the time to spend on explaining it all to them and why. Or that, you know, (how children are) with parents. If you bug [parents] long enough they get so sick of you that they'll let you do what you want.

Q Is that it?

A He wants to do something that he thinks may be more fun, rather than the tutorial which may be a little more work for him.

Q It would seem a waste of time?

A Yes. The amount of time that you can spend ... Well, if you let yourself fall into that trap – of negotiating and if he ends up having to do something that he really doesn't want to do, is he going to be serious about it, or is he just going to play around...?

Q So already that kid has to be watched...?

A Yes. He's trying to signal he is resistant to this learning activity and I think you've got to do something about that. Is he going to get anything meaningful out of what you want him to do?

Q So...?

A It isn't stressful because that's such a typical situation – we do that all the time.

Q Nothing new as far as computers go?

A Yes.

Q So in a sense you're saying kids often want to do something that they would rather do, that you don't want them to do, and there is nothing special there for computers – there's no extra edge here in the sense that...?

A Right, it's probably even less stressful because almost anything they do on computers they enjoy, and so it's not even as hard as, well, instead of writing extra spelling words three times each, you know. They'd rather do a spelling bee or something. As long as it's on the computer, they are going to enjoy it more than other choices. So, even if you give way, they are going to get something out of it.

Q So, even if you let them do it on the computer, their attitude is better?

A Yes, their attitude is better towards any task involving the computer than if they have to do something that's the regular.

Q So, even though they do a tutorial on the computer, the edge is off of it. If you're going to do spelling words – that's really boring.

A Yes, so he'd say, well OK, if you don't want to do it on the computer, how about you just go back and do your seat work instead. Well then, they will decide to stay on the computer.
   [Laughter]

Q I'm just wondering what's at stake for you as a teacher when a [student disagrees with an answer given by the computer]?

A I'm thinking of somebody who doesn't have much background, either working with a computer or knowledge of the computer programming. If there's a flaw, the teacher may not be able to diagnose where it went wrong. You are exposing your ignorance of working with computers, and you're no longer the source of knowledge for the child that they expected you to be – [to have] that credibility.

Whereas in most other subjects in the classroom, if they run into a difficulty with something in the textbook, you can always put the pages back. You're likely to be so familiar with all of that work that you've got the right answer ready, and if they are working on a fraction problem you can spot [the problem] immediately.

Q You can't back it up? Is it that?

A Well, if you're not conversant with how a computer operates you may not even know where breakdowns can occur, and then you would be totally lost.

Q Right. Well, this may not be a breakdown. It could be just a situation where the kid didn't get the right answer. Look it up in the back of the maths book – answer doesn't agree, sort of thing. That can happen.

A Yes. But then you could probably work it our yourself pretty quickly and see what the problem is.

Q Right.

A But with computer work you may not always have the background knowledge to be able to do it.

Q Unless you know the tutorial problem very well.

A Right.

Q In which case you might [be able to work it out].

A Yes.

Q Or am I putting words in your mouth?

A No. That's what I meant. Just a very simple thing – like you misread a direction, or you punched in the wrong number or something.

Q Yes and that's . . .

A And then you get just a little bit uptight, because if you don't solve this problem this whole thing is going to be lost and secondly, you just feel a little more threatened because you're so used to being able to solve problems, that now when you can't you . . .

Q Yes – I have the same feeling with my daughter's Grade 9 maths problems sometimes. Is it like that? When you can't dodge back and . . .

A Yes. Because I think we're all at the stage where we have competence in areas that we're quite used to and that we can handle quite well and being able to pass along.

Q Yes. So this may be a special edge on the computer that's newish.

A Yes.

A student wanting to play a game instead of working isn't new. Children are always nagging teachers to do something else, and now they want to do things with computers – tutorials on the computer are better than being back at one's seat working on similar activities. This negotiation, however, may end up with students wasting time. The child who has signalled his disinterest with the regular work has to be watched. The student may be working at the computer but how does the *teacher* know that the student is getting anything out of it, especially those students who the teacher knows need to be monitored. Usually the teacher can monitor these students quickly and at a distance. Ms Manuel says monitoring isn't easy when computers are involved because it isn't that clear *where* the student is at.

We asked Ms Manuel why she feels there is a risk when the student disagrees with an answer the computer gives. Furthermore, how is she to help students when problems arise?

When a student is stuck it isn't immediately clear to her whether there is a machine problem or a problem with the content. This ambiguity about the computer makes it difficult for her to monitor what students are doing and more difficult to know how to help them. Her very capacity to diagnose problems and prescribe remedies is brought into question.

We saw that Ms Manuel focuses on a potential technical problem when asked about a student who had come up with an answer that diverges from the 'book'. But it isn't a book but a computer that the student is working with and Ms Manuel feels at risk because she is unable to go back into the 'book' and see what is wrong. A book doesn't 'crash' when you write down the wrong answer – this can happen with computers because the right answer turns the 'pages' of the computer. Often you can't turn the pages back if you don't get the answer right – you can't look back; it is buried in the program. The computer is a black box and you can't look inside. Ms Manuel values her capacity to help her students – finding out if they are stuck and seeing how they can be unstuck. The computer represents a new kind of 'stuckness' and requires a level of monitoring more intense and demanding than Ms Manuel normally has to engage in. To be helpful she has to be quite close up to what the student is doing and even then there is no guarantee that she'll be able to spot the problem. At risk here isn't only her actual capacity to help, but the perceptions her students have of her of being someone they can rely on.

Q [You see] a student report [as a] risk for you. Why is that?
A It wouldn't bother me because I like to give them lots of opportunities where they can shine at something and have the chance to show leadership.
Q It generally fits into your work?
A Oh yes. If you can't do something yourself, get somebody who can.
Q Right. It's just occasionally I suspect there are some feelings that . . . ?
A Well, you think that you [as the teacher] should find out more about this, and then it's frustrating because you don't have the time or the inclination – or the aptitude.
Q Right – it's the mental set.
A Right. Kids tend to pick it [using computers] up and you think, maybe if I

made more of an effort on that I would. This doesn't bother me that much. I know of other people who really get uptight about that kind of thing.

Q It's not a thing to do with young teachers/old teachers either?

A No, because it is a difference in aptitude and interests. I'd be willing to venture that the people who have done the least to develop themselves and who have the narrowest frames of interest in their own lives are the ones who are most threatened by anyone else showing any kind of expertise in a subject that they don't have, and yet they don't make any effort to further themselves in it too.

Q Computers may affect this.

A Well, computers will make it even worse.

Q Students asking for more of the work to be based on the computer, and students giving reports on their computer work seem to be similar events in your perception. Are they?

A Yes.

Q Where the kids are showing off, and these kids who *are* saying give us more maths work on the computer, what might be similar?

A Well, the teacher may not be able to [give more work] because she doesn't have the skills and the programming, or access to the material there.

Q You're on the spot?

A You're on the spot, right. You're somewhat at risk because you're so used to being able to hand out all kinds of dittos and you've got maths questions all ready.

Q Yes?

A Yes, right here – some problems to solve, but now you're asked for something in another area, and you're not prepared.

Q Your racket has no string.

A Right.
[Laughter]

Q So the kids who want more maths work – are these perhaps the same kids who are showing off their programming?

A Well, if they are the ones who can do it, then I'd say OK. Let's see what you can do.

Q Make your own program?

A Yes, go ahead.

Q [However] It could be that they're the ones who are challenged and motivated and very competent, or they just want to play some more on the computer? And that's where wasting time comes to light. It depends on the students involved and the motivations. Even if they're the ones who are the game players and who want more maths, I look at that positively, because they could do a lot of maths drills, you know, without thinking that it was drudgery.

Q And the computer which adds that little bit extra?

A Yes, and the computer [has things] for the television generation – lots of action and intricate play. And you're involved, yes – liven up the program and it makes it more fun for them. It has to be fun – nothing can be hard work and drudgery.

Q I just wonder if there's that little extra added edge with the computer?

A It feeds that urge to have fun, but you can't really deliver all that. Because you don't have enough time and they still have to be agile to go through those steps. And it requires a certain amount of patience – if you don't work through the required number of steps the thing doesn't work.

Q That's right. And then they get frustrated.

A And they get frustrated – right, or they say they're bored because, it turns out that they had to work through all these steps.

Q They thought it was going to be fun, but it turns out not to be fun for them. So you've got a double problem.

A Yeah. They're expecting fun and they have to go through all these other steps before they get anything out of it.

Q It sounds like a bind for the teacher.

A Yes.

Q You know that – Give us more, but don't give us more. Because we're suddenly finding out that we have to work.
[Laughter]

How does she cope with this machine? Familiar routines are extended to make use of the computer and students are monitored as before. Rewards are distributed as usual, some children show off their special talents and students make unacceptable demands and equipment still has to be fixed.

Although Ms Manuel indicated that there was a risk attached to students giving a report she prefers to think that such a report is simply another example of students showing and telling. Yet the computer clearly represents a technical challenge to her and other teachers. The demand for more mathematics on the computer raises questions of skills in developing material. Supplying computer experiences isn't the same as giving out dittos (hand outs), as she puts it aptly. The students who are the computer whizzes are putting pressure on the teacher to liven things up. The computer caters to the students' desire to have fun; but there is a twist in the tail as Ms Manuel sees it. There are the 'steps' to go through in computer-assisted learning and they require patience. It isn't all fun, and some are going to be frustrated and so there may be a backlash. The computer-oriented students may find that the fun they had hoped for isn't there. The computer makes demands on them to get the steps right – just as it demands that Ms Manuel get them right.

We can see how the computer challenges the teacher's conception of her role. Is the work she is giving lively enough for the 'television generation'? Will she be able to use effectively the software available to her? Will she still be able to help students when they are stuck? Will her existing routines be able to cope? Most fundamentally, she is asking herself how adequate her routines are. What messages about learning is she conveying to her students through her teaching? Is she able to satisfy the demands of this computer-oriented generation?

Case Study 3: New games in Ms Melville's classroom

We can see how classroom routines are challenged by innovation by considering the case of Ms Melville – a geography teacher. She participated with us in a study of how she and others adapted computers to classroom life (Olson and Eaton 1986). We joined Ms Melville's class doing a unit on primary resources in a section on mining in the Canadian geography course using the *OIL SEARCH* program.

In *OIL SEARCH* students work in a group which starts with $900 capital to obtain information about the nature of the strata underlying its land, or to pay for drilling. The students can ask for a seismic study, a rock density analysis, or a core sample which will give them the information about the oil potential of their land needed to decide to drill. They can, at any time, decide to sell their oil in order to fund further search and drilling activities. This was the second time she had done *OIL SEARCH*. She knew what to expect:

> In order to find the oil, they had to learn the concepts. They had to know different types of oil traps, and they had to know what kind of rock to look in. They learned that better than my sitting up there saying: 'Okay, this is an oil trap. This is what it looks like. Let's copy it down.' They knew if they didn't know what it was they were going to miss where the oil was. It was competitive.

Ms Melville described how, on the first day, the noise level had been high – the students were excited about doing it because they had heard about it from the previous year's students. By the third lesson, which we taped, the change-overs were smooth and relatively quiet.

> You've got to have something else to keep them busy in between rather than just the computer program because it doesn't keep them busy. If they have something else that's related, a set of exercises of some sort, then they keep themselves busy.
>
> They work quite well in groups. You always get the odd one. One kid was a Little Hitler, literally. He was going to do it his way, but fortunately in the group there were others who were not quite as strong, but equally as persuasive in a nice way. That group had problems but it was mainly the make-up of the group, and I didn't know the kids that well at the beginning, and that was very close to the beginning. I didn't know how they interacted on a normal basis.
>
> By the third lesson I was not called upon that often; the groups simply pressed on with the problem of finding oil. There was a lot of argument

in one group, however, because they could not agree how to proceed. I had to put them back on track. One group were having difficulty plotting their graph and I went over to help. I was monitoring the group that was not doing well and went over to them to ensure that the students were able to capitalize on useful information that would soon lead them to oil. I did not want them to 'blow it'.

Finally a group found oil and much excitement was heard from their computer corner. They had found an oil trap and had to map exactly where it was. But they would have to wait until the next day to drill and finally hit oil and Ms Melville wanted to make sure they did not lose the spot.

Later, when *OIL SEARCH* was over, the class discussed what they thought about the simulation and what they learned about the techniques of oil drilling and the economics of the process. Ms Melville taped that discussion for us. The students made a number of points about the real world connections of the simulation and how unrealistic the price of oil was in the program.

We asked her to construe her experience of teaching with computers using the grid technique we had used with Mr Coulomb and Ms Manuel (see Table 2). She said that playing with computers was a legitimate element of what students were doing on the computers but time was a problem because the programs take longer to cover the same material and there is still all the other material in the curriculum to be covered.

> When the students are first starting on the program and you've got six computers going, the problem is they do not read the information. If they would read the information they wouldn't have that problem. If one of the other kids comes over and says: 'Did you read that?', it's much more effective than if I say it.
>
> They see the program [and say]: 'That's great!'. Put the disk in: 'Tremendous, let's go!' It's a general problem and I think it gets better with maturity. It's a skill they can learn from computers. There is nothing wrong at the grade 9 level with expecting a kid to be able to follow instructions, provided they are well-stated. That can be a problem too. [Then] if you don't do it, you don't get anywhere. The [advanced students] are just as bad as the [less able ones]. It's got to a point where students are saying to each other: 'Did you read it?'
>
> Now this girl did it last year, she's repeating. She knows the procedure and she has been good for them [the boys in her group] because they tend to be clowns. She's keeping them on track. It's a good responsibility for her. It's good for her self-confidence. She's guiding those two characters and they are getting somewhere.

Machine problems are less of a difficulty than student behavioural problems, because a program problem is easier to deal with than the more ambiguous student problem in working at the computer. You never know what the kids are going to do but the computer is pretty reliable.

Students helping other students is not a problem because students more readily accept help from peers: when they are stuck on the computer they know who in the class can get them 'unstuck'. Without these knowledgeable students Ms Melville said that things would be more hectic. Problems students have with computers are ambiguous and hectic. She has to think about them more than she would a simple mechanical failure. The unexpected problems to do with what the students are learning make things hectic; not the expected things, like the noise. As students become more familiar and confident with the computers, things do become less hectic, but individual problems still arise. Why a student is in trouble still needs to be diagnosed, and doing that is difficult, she said.

She said that they have to learn the value of reading the material; although sometimes they have to be left to learn it for themselves. Some deliberately ignore instructions and 'play' with the program. For example, in the farming game students grew potatoes in southern Ontario for ten years and made a lot of money, but making money was not the point of the exercise. They did not learn the geographical lesson and so were wasting their time on the computer, she said.

They also have to read the support documents carefully and find the information. Less able students do not do this. At first the groups were too big; now she has them working in pairs because, 'they don't have the confidence with the machines that some of the other kids have'. For some students, working in groups is a good thing.

Having a computer in her room creates situations which are ambiguous, take time to sort out, and press upon her. There is no quick way around these situations. She has to move into close contact with the students, find out what the problem is and sort it out. She wishes that students would sort things out for themselves. Normally teachers can rely on students to do that just using textbooks and other carefully 'scripted' materials. Not with computers.

Computer-based learning, however, disrupts that assumption and de-rails routines based on students' ability to follow instructions within a known framework. Moving out of the known framework, in which the significance of activity is unambiguous, to the computer framework is difficult. The students have difficulty because they do not *read* the instructions, but they also have difficulty because the learning activity itself takes place in an unfamiliar context. Well known routines which give significance to instructions do not exist, and students have to depend on the teacher to tell them in what direction to move. A new game with new rules takes time to understand.

Routines are very important to the teacher and the student. For the student, they provide a context for action; for the teacher, a basis for coping with large numbers of students without having to give individual tutorials. The routine is the context in which the teacher can exert influence – it is the context in which students can make sense of what the teacher is asking of them. Routines take the place of tutorials. A tutorial is a way of placing activity into context – of giving meaning to instructions. Tutorials which concentrate only on the cognitive demands of an activity, while ignoring the need to place activity in a meaningful context, do not work well.

Teachers provide a complex system of cues that help students stay on the right track. It is Ms Melville's teaching purpose which provides the context for *OIL SEARCH*, not the program itself, and it is to her that students come in order to get guidance. Or to the students who had done it before – who knew what things signify.

This is not to say that her purposes are not problematic. Ms Melville struggles with both the fundamental ambiguities of computers, but especially the question: just what is this technology for? Take her attitude to 'playing' with the computer.

The question of play is very much a part of what these teachers care about. Ms Melville, for example, does not like the students to 'play' with the computer. They are not seeing the computer in the same way she is. Their 'play', which for some would be exactly what the students should be doing, is not what the computer is for. The computer is to help her teach the basic facts of the subject in a more interesting way. Yet she is disappointed that students did not go beyond the facts to larger issues, doing what is essentially 'playful' – something she does not encourage. What her routine approach 'says' about what she believes is at odds with her espoused beliefs. This tacit conflict of purposes is challenged by the computer in her classroom.

Ms Melville has ritualized school work as a form of text 'worship' in which the serious business of getting messages from the text helps students become responsible through sustained and patient application. This 'worship' of text is part of the expressive dimension of her routines. She makes sure that her students understand how serious the text is and they in turn, knowing this, apply themselves. The computer introduces a new element into the process which upsets the serious work at the text – the computer encourages 'play' and inattention to text. It invites activities which are 'playful' and which could, were she not so concerned about the text, support more free flowing discussion and inquiry learning. She says she wants to do that kind of teaching, but her belief in the importance of text is at odds with this more 'playful' approach. As yet she doesn't know how to use this playful approach.

One might think that these teachers would not want to continue with computers, yet they were eager to. Why? Here we have an apparent paradox which we felt ought to be resolved. In spite of the fact that their efforts to incorporate computers into existing routines did not work as well as they hoped, they were prepared to continue with this way of teaching the subject. They found that students enjoyed the computer-based learning in spite of its difficulties. Teachers felt that the difficulties were worth the trouble because they enjoyed the students' pleasure at having a computer in their room. The teachers construed the using a computer as their way of being 'modern', of expressing something about the kind of teacher they were. This purpose seemed to overrule the evidence that their chosen way of teaching about a new subject had not worked out that well. Their mild disquiet about the routines was countered by the thought that their students had made significant gains using computers.

Why did teachers view computers in this positive way? The teachers spoke about the positive impact having a computer had on the class; how students were eager to use it; how much they enjoyed having it in the room. By having a computer in their room these teachers were able to say something about their interest in modern teaching methods and in the needs of their students, and about the relevance of their classroom to life outside it. The eight case studies reveal a common concern about the values inherent in using computers in the classroom. An analysis of the routines these teachers adopt tell us about what they value. These values are tacit – they are inherent in the routines and are the purposes to which the routines are directed. Understanding these purposes helps us understand the routines themselves.

However, often teacher routines are seen in a negative light. Teachers are often said to do things in an unconsidered way; the very idea of teacher routine activities, for example, suggests for some that consideration is absent. There is reason to doubt this idea. Although teachers may not always be able to tell us 'what was in their mind' when doing this or that, we would be wrong to assume that something unconsidered was going on. On the contrary, we might think that routines express what teachers know how to do and why they do it. We ought to think of routines more as the centre of what teachers do, rather than activities of a simple or unconsidered kind, even though the meaning and significance of routines remains tacit. We have to recover that meaning and significance if we are to understand what teaching is about and how it can improve. What must we attend to in order to recover the meaning of classroom routines? Let us consider three elements of the tacit dimension of practice that can illuminate it. They are: knowing how and knowing that; the intentions of teachers; and the person as meaning maker. A discussion of these elements provides us with a basis for interpreting the tacit dimension of practice – a process we will consider in the next chapter.

3

Understanding the tacit dimension of practice

Teachers often have been accused of rather simplistic conceptions of what they do. Their practice has been seen to be weak and in need of bolstering especially by extracting solid prescriptions from the social sciences. We ought to consider carefully studying *practice* to decide what teachers can actually do. That teachers may not be able to give a well articulated propositional account of their practice is another problem. They may or may not.

Not 'thinking' about teaching as they do it does not stop teachers from efficient practice and while it may be a good thing for them to be able to articulate well what they are doing, that doesn't stop them doing it well.

The capacity to talk about practice and to practice are different things. If we want to study teacher practice – what teachers know how to do – we have to observe what they do. We may be interested in how they explain or justify what they do; how their knowledge is articulated retrospectively. Let us not mistake one for the other or collapse the both into the one. Their know 'that' performance is one thing; their know 'how' performance is another. Both are teacher actions we would like to know more about so that we might understand teachers and teaching better and to understand how teachers come to change their practice.

This line of thinking leads us to be concerned about what teachers do as well as what they say about what they do, and to be careful about how we judge their work as a whole. It could be dangerous, for example, to stress some theory about how teachers do what they do and then go ahead and look for evidence of such a theory in action. We might end up by proposing that teachers ought to do it the way theory says, and we would only be assessing what they do in reference to the hidden norm put up by theory. Take the case of teacher planning. As Ryle (1949) suggests, 'People do not plan their arguments before constructing them. Indeed if they had to plan what to think before thinking it they would never think at all; for this planning would itself be unplanned' (p. 30). Yet some of the research on teacher routines seem to assume that this is exactly what teachers do or ought to do. Perhaps the research is really a norm in disguise. If teachers are not planning before action then they should be, is the message of the research, and moreover they should do this according to particular theoretical models for planning. Yet why should they plan before acting when they already know how to act?

Polanyi (1958), in his book *The Study of Man*, picks up Ryle's concern about knowing *how* and knowing *that* in his distinction between *tacit* knowledge and *articulate* knowledge. Tacit knowledge is akin to know how. As Polanyi says, our powers of knowing 'operate widely without causing us to utter any explicit statements and even when they do issue in an utterance this is used merely as an instrument for enlarging the range of tacit powers that originated it' (p. 27).

Prearticulate knowledge, or tacit knowledge, we gain through experience. We learn about a new region by walking through it without maps. Our knowledge may never be articulate yet we can find our way around. We may learn to perform many activities without any articulation of them. Our knowing preceded our thinking about knowing. Tacit knowledge precedes articulate knowledge. This is also Ryle's point. Efficient practice precedes the theory of it.

Polanyi goes on to make another distinction about human knowing – the idea of *focal* and *subsidiary* awareness. This distinction is crucial to his idea of how we come to understand the actions of people, and to how we ought to view the details of their behaviour (e.g. classroom routines). He argues that the particulars of behaviour make sense only if we understand their purpose. He notes that words, graphs, maps and symbols are never objects of our attention in themselves, but pointers towards the things that they mean. Symbols can serve as instruments of meaning only by being known indirectly or *subsidiarily* while we fix the *focus* of attention on their meaning and their purpose. The same is true of tools and machines. Their meaning lies in their purposes. This is the way we have to think about classroom routines.

Teacher intentions

Understanding of what people are doing cannot be had through mere examination of the particulars of their behaviour; we have to appreciate what they do in terms of what they are intending to accomplish. We have to understand their behaviour as pointers towards the *purposes* which they serve, and in terms of those purposes. The meaning of what people do lies in the purposes served by those actions. Hence, *isolated* actions are not objects of attention in themselves but indicators, known not in themselves, but subsidiarily to the purposes they serve.

In themselves they mean nothing. On this view, accounts of what teachers do which reduce teaching to isolated behavioural elements seem bound to fail for lack of a context to make sense of them. Such a focus guarantees that we will not really understand the meaning of isolated acts. Only a holistic view will do. Such a view is largely absent from research on teacher practice.

What people *know* how to do is bound up in *what* they do, and the meaning of what people do has to be understood in terms of the purposes they are attempting to achieve. Without understanding those purposes we cannot understand what the actions mean. Schon (1983), in his book *The Reflective Practitioner*, also criticizes the idea that theory precedes practice, and that the intelligence lies in the theory not in practice. He mounts the same critique of this idea as do Ryle and Polanyi. He takes issue with what he calls the 'model of technical rationality'. This model, he says, assumes that professional activity consists in 'instrumental problem solving made rigorous by the application of scientific theory and technique'. Science he says, does not tell us how to identify purposes. The process of identifying purposes cannot be reduced to a technique. There are no such techniques.

Schon adopts the idea that knowing is inherent in action and that the challenge for understanding and improving professional practice is to make articulate what is inarticulately embodied in action itself. The starting point for improvement is practice, not norms derived from social sciences; although the findings of social sciences might have some bearing on the critique of practice once articulated. Practice itself, he says, is knowledgeable. More is done in our practice than we can say. For Schon, to educate the professional is to engage him/her in making the tacit articulate and to subject that to criticism. But how should we go about this? The examples Schon gives suggest an *historical* approach to understanding practice – a critical reflection on the meaning of one's actions in their historical context. This is the view that Polanyi takes.

Rather than fundamental differences between the study of history and natural science, Polanyi sees simply differences in the degree to which we identify with the subject matter being studied. He sees a progression of identification from the inanimate to the animate to man. The need for identification is greatest when the object of study is man, and greatest in the study of history – in the study of human action which is what we are concerned about here. I want to pursue the significance of the idea of *identification* with teachers as it bears on our efforts to understand teacher routines.

Polanyi suggests, first, that we recognize the biological and cultural rootedness of free action; second, that we assume that all humans have free access to standards of truthfulness and are obliged to limit actions in relation to them in all times, and that, third, we assume that the human mind is the seat of responsible choices. While people may fail, they have the capacity to succeed and the access to truth which will help them succeed. This is where Polanyi wants to lodge his study of man. I think it may be a good place to lodge the study of teacher routines.

Practically speaking, how do we come to understand other people's actions? Polanyi suggests that we have to participate in the life of the person we want to know. We have to identify with the person:

> This we do anyway when we study other things, but it reaches a point with man that when we arrive at the contemplation of a human being as a responsible person and we apply to him the same standards as we accept for ourselves, our knowledge of him has definitely lost the character of an observation and has become an encounter instead.
>
> (Polanyi 1958: 95)

Instead of the atomistic approach to understanding people's action that I spoke of earlier, Polanyi urges us to understand actions in their context. In other words he points to an holistic approach to interpretation.

Polanyi uses the term 'in-dwelling' to suggest the kind of attention to the other person that we should strive to achieve. This view has much in common with an approach to understanding other people developed by George Kelly (1955) which has been used as a research tool in the case studies we have been considering in this chapter.

The person as meaning maker

It is interesting to note that George Kelly, through critical reflection on his *own* clinical practice and his own know-how, produced an articulation of that practice which became his personal construct theory. Kelly's work might be seen as a way of creating the kind of personal encounter that Polanyi considers so important. By rendering the tacit knowledge articulate we can gain the advantage of being able to discuss practice, and to subject *know how* that is in practice to critical scrutiny.

Kelly himself, as a clinician, was very interested in finding ways to help people articulate what they did and why they did it. He recognized how difficult it is to move from doing things to knowing what one is doing and why. His grids are aids to the accomplishment of such a process; they are the means to achieve the 'in-dwelling' of the clinician that Polanyi speaks of.

The philosopher Theodore Mischel (1964) points out that Kelly's theory may be regarded as a guide to careful listening. The listening is aimed at uncovering the *reasons* why people behave as they do. Mischel, in fact, reconstructs Kelly's theory in terms of *constructs as reasons*, not as anticipations of plans. Constructs he sees channelling behaviours because they are the rules or reasons which people follow in their behaviour. The use of grids and the conversations that go with them might be seen as means to articulate the reasons that are embedded in people's actions.

Constructs do not tell us about our anticipations, they tell us about what is built into our actions as we act. They are an expression of the intentions that guide and channel our behaviour. We simply plunge ahead tacitly acting out what we know until, of course, something gives us pause and we begin to reflect on our actions in an effort to make articulate what is tacit – to construe our behaviour. This is the way I would read what Kelly is saying. On this view Kelly offers us a powerful method for trying to help people articulate for us what is the meaning of their actions – what intentions guide and channel behaviour?

Kelly's constructive approach to change involves relationships between insiders, people carrying out their tasks, and outsiders. Its approach is clinical: advice is offered, but in a way that respects the intentions of the teacher. Too many approaches foreclose on what teachers might consider salient in favour of 'objective' evidence of behaviour. Peters and White point out that:

> External observation is not quite enough; the student has to enter imaginatively into the phenomena in question if he is to make sense of them. The anthropologist describing the behaviour of a primitive tribe, the psychiatrist studying schizophrenia, have to understand the conceptual schemes of the tribesmen or the schizophrenic from the inside. For human actions are not simply bodily movement . . . their identification normally depends on identifying the intention behind them.
>
> (Peters and White 1973: 104)

Similarly Fenstermacher (1978) notes: 'In cognitive psychology and in information processing theory, the thoughts and feelings of persons are used as clues to understanding developmental and information processing structures' (p. 180). This is the same point that Mancuso and Eimer (1980) make:

> The mechanists' search for universally-categorized psychological stimuli has failed, even when that search has been focused on a central category such as praise. For context must be considered if one seeks to explain the effects of one or another stimulus, and the context of any behaviour includes the construction systems of persons who anticipate in the psychological event.
>
> (Mancuso and Eimer 1980: 39)

As we have seen the search for mechanism short circuits rather than a search for mechanisms, we need to understand the behaviour in terms of what the teachers are trying to do. As Pope (1978) points out:

> Emphasis on the person-as-meaning-maker is now a dominant theme in educational theorizing, but in practice, the phenomenological world is often neglected. However, there are some who do stress the need for teachers to become aware of the personal constructs or 'alternative

frameworks' which students bring with them to science lessons. Some of these explicitly refer to Kelly's notions whilst others appear to be Kellyian in spirit.

(Pope 1978: 8)

Lortie (1975) draws our attention to this idea of the person-as-meaning-maker:

> Educational goals are often stated in global, even Utopian terms . . . [We] observed that teachers 'reduce' such goals into specific objectives they use in their daily work. This reduction apparently involves two consecutive tendencies; relying on personal convictions and obtaining high satisfaction from outcomes that are less than universalistic. When teachers cannot use stated goals to guide their actions, organizational objectives give way to personal values; the personal values, as we saw . . . are heavily influenced by past experience.
>
> (Lortie 1975: 212)

Lortie suggests that teachers 'reduce' the global to the personal because the personal makes more sense and is more satisfying. Teachers 'conserve' personal values and satisfactions in the face of more universalistic expectations because they are coping with work demands which are difficult to understand and with consequences of actions which are hard to foresee. Thus, for example, anticipating the effects of a particular teaching approach allows teachers to assess and make choices; and the significant point is that these choices tend to preserve the more delimited and satisfying elements of teaching at the expense of the more universalistic expectations of the curriculum developers and other outsiders (Olson 1980).

We must consult the views of teachers if we want to understand why they make the choices they do. In this way we can understand what their actions mean within their system of thought, and we have to know that system as a whole if we are to understand the meaning of their actions.

Those involved in educating others are engaged in a morally bound pursuit and act as moral agents. It does not therefore seem possible, on the one hand, to accept that what teachers do is bound up in the resolution of issues whose roots are moral and, on the other, to ignore the views of teachers in an attempt to understand how that agency is accomplished.

Problems that teachers face are inadequately understood and, combined with an inadequate conception of the meaning of teacher behaviour, there have been unrealistic expectations of rapid change in school practice. These exceptions have been based on a 'mechanical' model of the interaction between teachers and forces which either press for change or inhibit it. But most teachers do not do the kinds of things for which a mechanical model of their work is appropriate. What they do is sufficiently complex ethically and practically to require a more humane perspective. In view of the complexity of the tasks and differing value positions associated with education, it is hard to see how the image of teacher as target of manipulation can serve.

Now this view coincides with an eloquent expression of it by Kelly in slightly different terms. As Kelly says:

> There are two ways in which one can look at psychological measure-
> ment and clinical diagnosis ... seek to fix the position of the subject
> with respect to certain dimensions or coordinates ... or classify him
> as a clinical type or ... concern himself with the subject's freedom of
> movement, his potentialities, the resources which can be mobilized ...
> From the point of view of personal construct theory the latter represents
> the more enlightened approach.
>
> (Kelly 1955: 203)

Such a view is central to the constructive approach – understanding how other people make sense of their world. To do this, the collaborator has to remain still long enough to understand the status quo – that is, to understand how people think about their work as it is now rather than hustle them onward to new visions.

When schools and teachers are asked to change, this occurs in a context which is already functioning to accomplish goals. Traditions already exist which become targets for change. The fact that these traditions exist ought to interest people who want school to change. Lortie makes a similar point in relation to assessing the effects of computer-assisted instruction (CAI):

> It is one thing to make general assertions about the differences between
> human and man-made interactions, but quite another to identify and
> measure their effects on students. To do so we must dig deeper into
> previously ignored aspects of the conventional situation, thus probing
> aspects of schooling which were previously ignored. This is indicative
> of the general tendency to change to increase our interest in the status
> quo.
>
> (Lortie 1973: 478)

How are we to understand the status quo? To do so House (1974) suggested that it is necessary to understand the phenomenology of the teacher's world. As Kelly (1955) put it: 'Two people can act alike even if they have each been exposed to quite different phenomenal stimuli. It is in the similarity in the construction of events that we find the basis for similar action and not in the identity of the events themselves' (p. 91).

Research in education has tended to look at school and classroom events from the viewpoint of the outsider, whose construction of school life may, in practice, have limited points of contact with those of the teachers. Outsiders may simply not be in a position to understand what practice means to insiders, nor what any proposed changes might mean. This kind of arrogant acceptance of the view of the outsider is criticized by Reid (1979), who notes:

'Research [of this kind] is something done by the expert to the inexpert. [In such a process] people who are the actual objects of research are the last to be consulted. Clearly the views of the "insiders" must be consulted' (p. 168).

As an approach to understanding the view of insiders, Hudson (1975) argues for a 'hermeneutic' approach to evidence in which the interpreter either reconstructs another person's intentions using that other person's terms, or restructures that other person's intentions in some new terms. These interpretations start with the other person.

In this process some statements are more important than others; the outsider has to know what are the important elements of other people's ideas and then work to preserve the meaning of these in the interpretation. To know what these elements are, he or she has to know the rationale of the overall system of beliefs. We can't know this unless we take seriously the views of others we wish to help. In the next chapter we look at the central place of dilemmas in the practice of teaching and how those dilemmas can help us understand just what teachers face as they try to reconcile the many conflicting elements of their work. These dilemmas are not part of the surface events an outsider can witness – they are revealed when we take the process of collaborating with teachers seriously – when we probe the tacit dimension of practice.

4

Tradition and the improvement of teaching

A holistic approach to teaching

Reflecting on the traditional routines of teaching is a way of understanding teaching better. But how can we appreciate what the tradition means? In this chapter we shall consider the holistic approach to the study of teaching which draws on the idea of tacit knowledge and leads us to consider how traditional classroom routines enable teachers to resolve, at least for the moment, basic dilemmas of teaching.

We began by looking at a holistic approach to teaching by drawing on the work of the ethnographer Clifford Geertz whose contribution to the interpretive approach to understanding human action is fundamental. Later in the chapter we shall see how the personal construct methods of George Kelly can be used to develop an understanding of the teacher's point of view. In the last chapter we will look in more detail at this way of analysing and evaluating practice.

As Geertz (1973) says, 'man is an animal suspended in webs of significance he himself has spun ... I take culture to be those webs and the analysis of it to be therefore not an experimental science in search of law but an interpretive one in search of meaning' (p. 5).

Teachers spin webs of significance every day in their classrooms: they encourage their students to enter into the world of learning that they create. The teacher, who is fluent in that world, wants students to be at home there. What kind of webs of significance do teachers spin and how can we understand them? Geertz argues that we need a 'thick' description of the events of our social lives. He says that:

> Culture consists of socially established structures of meaning in terms
> of which people do things ... what ... most prevents those of us ...
> from grouping what people are up to is not ignorance as to how cog-
> nition works ... as a lack of familiarity with the imaginative universe
> within which their acts are signs.
>
> (Geertz 1973: 13)

This getting to know what the acts signify is what we mean by thick description.

Social science need not be the only starting point for understanding practice. We could ask what teachers say through their work – ask what the
teaching we witness *means*. In such an approach we treat teaching acts as
'texts' to be understood – to be interpreted. This process involves what Geertz
calls 'thick description'.

Geertz (1973) didn't invent the term 'thick' description. In a lecture given
at the University of Saskatchewan, Gilbert Ryle drew a distinction between
thinner and thicker description of actions. To do this he asks the question
'What is *le Penseur* doing?' *Le Penseur* (the Thinker) is a famous statue by
the French sculptor August Rodin. 'What is the thinker really doing?' asks
Ryle. 'It is often supposed by philosophers and psychologists that thinking is
saying things to oneself ... But [this view] fails because it stops just where it
ought to begin ... What is the correct and thickest possible description of
what [he] was trying for in murmuring those syllables?' (p. 487). From a 'thin'
point of view the thinker is 'saying things to himself.' The description can be
thickened by reflecting upon his purposes in putting his chin on his hand,
and by considering his *situation* as a thinker. In short, we have to look
carefully at all we know about the thinker and try to invent a coherent story
that makes sense of what we know. We have to place the thinker in a situation
which is intelligible to us and to him (could he actually think). It isn't enough
to say he is muttering words to himself – thinking is more complex than that.

This kind of thick description is what we need for understanding teaching
acts. What might this thick description be like? When people do meaningful
things they depend upon a pre-existing structure to communicate their intention. This structure enables them to convey their meaning. Thick description
of teaching is the uncovering of the meaning of what is being said (done) by
knowing the structure in which it is said (done), and by knowing the 'language' in which it can be said.

As Geertz points out:

> Doing ethnography is like trying to read (in the sense of 'construct a
> reading of') a manuscript – foreign, faded, full of ellipses, incoheren-
> cies, suspicious emendations, and tendentious commentary, but written
> not in graph of sound but in transient examples of shaped behaviour.
>
> (Geertz 1973: 10)

The ethnography that Geertz argues for is not common in education.

We have, in the past, offered thin descriptions of teachers and then accused them of rather simplistic conceptions of what they do. Their 'thinking' has been seen to be weak and in need of bolstering, especially by giving them extracts from the social sciences. Lortie (1975), for example, says that the 'ethos of the profession is tilted against pedagogical inquiry.' Teacher theories, he says, are simple and uncritical. But is their *practice* itself so bereft of intelligence? Is their *know-how* so deficient? This is another matter, and I think the answer is no. The practice is much more skilful and intelligent than how teachers talk about it might indicate.

What teachers know is embedded in their *know-how*. It is only because of what Ryle (1949) calls the 'intellectualist legend', what might also be called the cognitivist model, that we tend to assess the intelligence of performance on the basis of the quality of the supposed cognitive events involved in planning. If we find that the operations are poorly articulated, we assume that the practice itself is also poor. Not so, says Ryle. These are two different things. He argues that contrary to the intellectualist legend, efficient practice precedes the theory of it, and intelligence is in the practice, not in the *thinking* about it. Abilities are played out in the practice itself – in the know-how. Teachers face difficulties when they have to teach without being able to rely on their know-how. What they say about those difficulties allows us insight into why teachers work as they do – into the purposes of their actions.

Teachers may not be able to give a well articulated, propositional account of their practice. But complex ideas about how to teach are embedded in the familiar routines of the classroom. Not 'thinking' about teaching does not stop teachers from efficient practice. While it may be a 'good thing' for them to be able to articulate well what they are doing, that doesn't stop them doing it well. Indeed talk about teaching routines as if they were relatively thoughtless is a 'thin' representation of them.

Comprehension of what another person is doing cannot be had through mere examination of the particulars of their behaviour (Polanyi 1958). We have to understand their behaviour as pointers towards the purposes which they serve, and in terms of those purposes. The meaning of what people do lies in the purposes served by those actions, which are not meaningful in themselves, but indicators of the purposes they serve which give them meaning. In themselves they mean nothing.

On this view, simply looking at isolated incidents in the classroom is bound to fail as a method for lack of a context to make sense of them. Such an image of humans as subjected to pushes and pulls of experience has already been criticized above. Kelly says, 'No one needs to paint himself into a corner; no one needs to be completely hemmed in by circumstances; no one needs to be the victim of his biography. We call this philosophical position *constructive alternativism*' (p. 15). He contrasts this position with that of the psycho-metrician: 'There are two ways in which one can look at psychological measurement and clinical diagnosis ... He can seek to fix the position of the subject with respect to certain dimensions ... (or) he can concern himself with the subject's freedom of movement, ... the resources which can be mobilized' (p. 203). Kelly's constructive alternativism is given operation in terms of his idea that people form constructs of similarity and contrast, and anticipate their experience of others by using such constructs. People, he argues, are ready for experience. What is going to happen is anticipated and the anticipation is based on previous experience.

People do not always either *want* to reveal their reasons for acting, or even *know* what they are consciously, although they may have tacit knowledge of them. How can we help them to find out what those reasons are? Kelly's method depends on people making distinctions about people or situations in which they find themselves on the basis of differences they see between elements representative of those people or the situations. Now, people are not always ready or able to make such distinctions; they may make apparently different distinctions which are, in fact, not different; or they may make apparently superficial distinctions. The point is emphasized by Bannister and Mair (1968) who note,

> One important point about constructs which is frequently misunder-stood is that many, perhaps most, constructs are not highly intellec-tualized with precise dimensions of discrimination, clearly and adequately expressed in words. Often a construct may be acted out in a tentative way rather than consciously appreciated and conceptualized by its users.
>
> (Bannister and Mair 1968: 29)

None the less, allowing people to make their own distinctions and to make them within a defined field represented by limited yet representative elements from that field is a potentially powerful way of gaining important insights into the perspective of the person. The person may not be aware of the deeper significance of the distinctions they are making and the inter-viewer, using the pattern of distinctions made by the person, has to make sense of it in the light of everything that the person has said about the field of experience under study.

We think we understand easily and clearly what happens in classrooms only because we think of teaching as an outcome of the application of psycho-logical principles. Once we see teaching as a thing itself – a social thing – it becomes much less clear that we know what is going on. It is only by constru-ing teaching as a technical process based on supposedly well-known rules that we have any security in thinking that we know what is going on. That security is only apparent – it is a chimera. Much more is going on than our focus of learning as a technical process would lead us to consider. What is going on isn't at all clear. Often those who have visions for schools fail to appreciate that.

Take the case of the British Schools Council Integrated Science Project. This is a project with a particular subject focus and format. None the less, it can stand as an example of a radical vision of a school subject which is created perennially. In order to stress that generic quality of the project, I shall refer to it herein as the radical vision as a way of contrasting it with the traditional practice it was meant to supplant.

The teachers that I spoke to raised matters that went well beyond the discovery learning which formed the basis of the radical vision (Olson 1982). They spoke of fundamental issues to do with classroom life and the climate which sustains it. They spoke about the basic securities and insecurities of their work in the school. Only in the light of these issues could I understand how they talked about their work and why they felt the way they did about the radical vision they were struggling with.

Schools working with the radical vision were chosen because, on the face of it, attempting to implement this particular project would pose a challenge to teachers, and thus teachers would likely want to talk about their work when faced with a number of problems of implementation. As can be seen from Table 4, the vision departed radically from the traditional practice of the schools.

Table 4 Radical vision and traditional teaching

	Radical vision	*Tradition*
Goals	General education Habits of critical intelligence Goals are tightly related to methods	Career orientation Acquisition of information Goals loosely related to methods
Classroom relationships	A new partnership between teachers and taught, equality Teacher–teacher co-operation	Teacher authority vested in subject expertise Teachers on their own
Pedagogy	Discovery approach Discussion Science as a process No syllabus No revision for exams Teacher control of content detail Internal assessment Attitude change assessed Assessment criterion referenced	Lecture/question–answer Instruction Science as content Syllabus based Revision for exams Mandated content No internal assessment No attitude change assessment Assessment norm referenced

Teachers valued and protected aspects of their work which had little to do with the discovery learning and its underlying theory of cognition. We found that equal shares of bright pupils, getting new equipment (even if not needed), and keeping faith with the collective definition of the subject were matters of paramount importance. These matters would not have surfaced had teaching been seen only as a cognitive process.

Coping with the demands of the vision was a fruitful context in which to talk to teachers about their teaching and specifically about how they resolved dilemmas associated with their use of the vision materials. Teachers were asked to discuss what they thought about elements of the project, to describe what problems they encountered in practice and to indicate how they resolved these problems. Students, administrators, project developers and supervisors were interviewed as part of the research design which also involved a survey of all teachers using the project.

It became clear from the interviews with the teachers and classroom observation that trying to implement the vision did indeed create dilemmas. Dilemmas arose when the theory of the vision was at odds with that of the teacher. Coping with these dilemmas became the basis for these teachers to talk about what their traditions meant to them and why the vision doctrine was upsetting. Invariably, dilemmas were resolved in favour of traditional routines. When asked to say how the dilemma was resolved, the teachers tended, initially, to say how the dilemma *might* be resolved, and this resolution was often in a direction opposite to how, later, they said it was resolved. These early efforts to preserve a 'front' were replaced by greater candour as the study progressed.

Understanding teaching experiences

The concept of a dilemma in curriculum is an important one for understanding the effects of visionary doctrine on practice. A dilemma is what teachers said they experienced because of a tension between traditional approaches to teaching and those new ones urged by the visionary doctrine. Westbury (1973) draws attention to the dilemmas associated with innovation: 'A vast gulf appears to separate the work place of the school, with their resources and tasks, from the kinds of work places reformers would want' (p. 152). This became clear from our observations in classrooms and from our interviews with teachers which were based on Kelly's work.

Kelly (1955) makes the point that 'the sharing of personal experience is a matter of construing the other person's experience and not merely a matter of having time to hand it across the desk. The psychology of personal constructs, therefore, lends itself quite conveniently to the handling of the theoretical problem of gaining access to private worlds' (p. 200). It is this sort of senti-

Table 5 Science teaching activities

1 Pupils are making notes during a lesson given by the teacher.
2 At their seats, pupils are doing problems.
3 The teacher is asking the class how to control an experiment.
4 The class is watching TV.
5 The teacher is asking pupils to offer hypotheses.
6 The teacher is doing a demonstration while pupils make observations.
7 In class some pupils are helping others who have had difficulty.
8 The teacher is questioning pupils to guide them to a generalization.
9 On a field trip to a pond pupils are collecting data.
10 The teacher is acting as neutral chairman in a class discussion.
11 The teacher is questioning the class on the homework.
12 The teacher is putting examples of a relationship on the board for the pupils' notes.
13 During a practical, pupils are making observations.
14 Three pupils are presenting a seminar.
15 The teacher is pointing out the scientific principles of a model he is demonstrating.
16 A group of pupils are gathering data from students on the sports field.
17 Pupils are writing an essay at home.
18 Pupils are making measurements to verify a law.
19 A pupil who has had difficulty is using a programmed text.
20 Pupils are supplying labels for a diagram.

ment that has guided the work of Kelly and makes his theories of the person relevant to this research. What Kelly has said can be interpreted to mean that people form rules to guide their behaviour, and that these rules are fashioned on the basis of how they have come to expect others to behave.

Each teacher in our research project grouped twenty teaching events which had been selected to reflect a range of roles and activities involved in science teaching (Table 5).

Afterwards began a free flowing discussion the aim of which was to help the person verbalize the basis of grouping. In this way the teachers could see themselves in classroom situations and talk about what they saw themselves doing and feeling in those situations. The discussion resulted in a form of words (the construct) which the person felt expressed the basis for assembling the grouping. To aid verbalizing of constructs, people were asked to contrast the group with an earlier group, or simply to express the significance of some comment made about the group.

Each construct (five elicited; five supplied) was placed at the top of a page which contained five spaces for the person to make an evaluation of each element in relation to each construct. The person was asked to decide to what extent a construct applied to each element in turn, or whether the construct did not apply at all. A final probing interview was scheduled during which each teacher discussed the way he/she filled in the grid with the investigator. The grid was a starting point for the teacher to discuss certain kinds of classroom situations which reflected more or less teacher control. The teachers explained apparent inconsistencies in their assessment of classroom events thus clarifying their decisions and providing a platform for further discussion.

Case Study 4: Radical visions in Ms Markle's science classroom

I'm going to create a composite picture of all of the teachers I talked to and call her Ms Markle. Through her voice we can appreciate what is at stake when classroom traditions are threatened. The comments of Ms Markle about teaching and the construct interview data indicated she felt she had lost influence in the classroom. Influence was undermined in the vision through having free ranging discussions in class, covering less and unfamiliar content in class and instructing outside her discipline. This loss of influence stemmed finally from the adoption by the project team of a complex model of cognition (Gagné 1965), as a basis for organizing the content and designing the intended classroom activities. These activities were explained in the project documents in an unfamiliar language of mentalistic events which were difficult for her to understand, let alone use as a basis for planning, teaching and evaluation activity. She was accustomed to talking about her teaching, not in terms of achieving levels of problem-solving skill, but in terms of notebooks accumulated and content learned as measured by mock and real examination results. The outcomes of the visionary approach were abstract – she looked for more tangible results.

She found her teaching and evaluation activities led to distressing classroom effects. Her traditional approaches were more reliable in accomplishing what she saw to be an unchanging goal of getting her students through an external examination and meeting parental, peer and administration expectations. Put simply, she faced a dilemma: a choice between persisting with visionary methods of exerting influence or retaining ones she could trust. However the choice was made, unsatisfactory consequences occurred. If she chose the former, she risked increasing the diffuseness of her role (Wilson 1962). If she chose the latter she risked not 'implementing' the vision, not stimulating the students intellectually and, perhaps, not preparing them properly for what she perceived to be an examination based on 'thinking' ability.

She resolved the dilemma in favour of tradition. She domesticated the vision. The project language was given new meaning in terms of tradition. Discussions, for her, became lectures or recitations and intellectual skill development was translated as content memorization and examination rehearsal. The integrated design translated as a patchwork of specialized content to be unravelled and resown, and criterion-referenced assessment was transformed into normative assessment. In short, after a period of experimentation during which she saw her influence declining, she re-established her influence through domesticating the vision.

A form of traditional teaching, what I call high teacher influence, could be seen in how she talked about her work. Traditional activities involved lecturing, note giving, seat work and other forms of transmitting and guaranteeing information, and creating attention and involvement. She exerted slightly less control when there was greater pupil participation, but she exercised firm control over the point and direction of the lesson, as in question–answer sequences, recitation and guided discovery.

Her influence serves a number of functions, the main one being that she can ensure a common basis of information for subsequent examination. Although she said that transfer of information did not engage the student intellectually, it was efficient for getting across facts without which, she said, further, more stimulating activity could not occur. While she emphasized that it was necessary to give notes and to lecture in spite of the drawbacks, she felt guilt about doing this prompted, perhaps, by her expectation that I would not approve of such methods, and by the fact that I came from the university and was investigating a project which stressed high *pupil* influence.

In her appraisal of her influence she used words like: fundamental; essential; have to have it; quick; economical; valid; necessary; productive. But associated with this emphatic, positive view of her influence were doubts. She realized that there was limited intellectual challenge for the student. She described her high-influence classroom activities as: menial; not ideal; rote; humdrum; the pupil as a sponge. The following descriptions of how she construed her influence illustrate the dilemmas she faced:

> Pupils sitting at their seats doing physics problems – that's menial, but it is essential ... Pupils supplying labels you don't really need, to understand what it's all about, to label a spade a spade sort of thing. You can do that and be successful at it, but have no idea what's going on. It's menial in that sense, but it is essential.
>
> I would never like to have a class sort of hung up too high and dry (with their) going out of the room thinking, 'Well, what on earth am I supposed to make of that one?'
>
> They've got to believe in what you are saying. If they think you are unsure of your facts, they switch off. Do they trust you are telling them the right things they need to know, and, in fact, is the stuff you are telling them factually correct?

She took her task to see that the lesson had a valid point and that the students could trust her to make sure that the class ended up with the right information and the correct ideas. Simultaneously, she had to ensure that the lesson did not go astray:

The teacher guides the discussion and puts them right if they are wrong. He takes out what isn't quite relevant.

Now the teacher is physiotherapist, putting right any of the ills.

The bulk of the lesson would be independent of the teacher, it's their feelings, but the crunch of the lesson is summing up; (this) would be the teacher.

The final arbiter of what is correct or incorrect is, I think, the teacher; unless someone else in the class knows the answer. I don't think kids naturally or automatically arrive at the right answer and of course the information they want is perhaps outside the range of experience, and therefore the teacher is very essential, very necessary.

Even though she conceded that the students ought to be allowed to discuss things amongst themselves, the real lesson began when she imposed her point of view. Thus, the low-influence lessons that formed an important part of the project were translated into high-influence ones, because she saw it as her job to make sure the point of the lesson was established. If the pupils on their own failed to get the point, then she had to step in. By acting as an editor, she served three related functions: students understand the material; they are assured that there is some point to understanding the material; and they participate in a process which is designed to engage their attention. By acting as an editor, even though not called upon to do so by the nature of the innovative materials, she is able to use methods more suited to her goal: preparing students for examinations. In spite of the cognitive orientation of the vision – the quest for generalized 'thinking skills' – this traditional function remained and she focused on it.

She also talked about steering the lesson to a desired end – a predictable outcome. This I have called the director function. Doing problems from a book or labelling a diagram had predictable outcomes because, through the materials, she controlled what pupils did. Such activities she saw as necessary and she contrasted them somewhat defensively with 'breaking new ground every time'; a reference to the supposed discoveries of the discovery approach which she didn't see happening in her class. She viewed practical work and demonstrations as a means of ensuring that the intended points would be made. The influence she can exert is captured by her emphatic language: 'If you are trying to get an important point over, you are going to choose an experiment which will show it. You don't choose something which might show it.'

By acting as a director she is able to ensure a relatively unambiguous role for herself. The point of the lesson was not left up in the air; what was to be learned clearly depended on moves she made before and during the lesson.

Teaching according to the vision

Ms Markle spoke quite differently about her normal teaching and what was expected of her according to the vision. Where she was clear about what she was trying to accomplish and how to go about it in the former case, she was unclear about the effects of her teaching and her role in the latter. Her comments about traditional teaching were definite, realistic and engaged. The comments about visionary teaching – discussion lessons, student seminars, essays, social issues lessons, or debates – were tentative, detached and unrealistic. All of these trends suggested that she had not adopted the approved cognitive language associated with the vision. It is not surprising, therefore, that she translated visionary activities into variants of the traditional high activity ones. Why did she end up translating the vision into tradition?

The teacher as translator

Before we consider how she translated the vision let us consider the difficulties she had making sense of it. Two sources can be seen to contribute to the lack of understanding of the vision with its emphasis on reduced teacher influence. First, she found it difficult to understand the cognitive model of the project and she did not accept the goals associated with low teacher influence. Her description of the cognitive model was vague and not related to what she actually did in the classroom. Secondly, she had difficulty in understanding what she or her pupils were meant to do in low influence teaching. Each of these points we now discuss in greater detail.

It was clear from the way she spoke about the mental events which were supposed to occur as a consequence of her reduced influence, that she did not understand what was meant by problem-solving and pattern-finding skills. The following phrases are illustrative:

> They are having information fed to them and they are having to churn some information back out again. It has to undergo a wavelength change.
>
> We then infer from the data. When the pupils are given or have the information, they are asked to deduce what might happen, what is what ... They have to have various ideas ... In putting labels (on a diagram) ... they are using previous notes and previous experiences and reasoning from them.
>
> Psychological strata are, ideally, all being brought into play here ... They must involve a variety of bringing together of all of your different affective and cognitive styles of thought.

These phrases suggest that she was groping for language to express the cognitive outcomes of her instruction. It is not surprising, then, that she was tentative when it comes to describing what happened to students as a consequence of reduced influence teaching.

The second reason that she finds it difficult to teach with reduced influence stems from her perplexity about teacher and student roles. Without a clear sense of mutual roles she is at a loss to know how to behave during low influence lessons. Low influence teaching seems to involve the abdication from teaching, as the following passage suggests:

> It's quite foreign to a lot of science teachers (being a neutral chairman). They deal with a lot of facts and here we are asking for discussions which could be very open-ended … It's very difficult to manage (a discussion) with some of them absent or some have the facts and some don't … Then you've got pupils at different levels of maturity to discuss something. Whereas some can and they might be mature enough to put forward certain views, but not in a mature manner, laughing about it, giving some stupid sort of view …

She used images of retreat and withdrawal, or abdication of the teacher role entirely:

> The teacher doesn't seem involved.
> The teacher is just a controlling person in the background, if necessary … The teacher is a guiding hand.
> I'm likely to be hovering, guiding, inspiring, ticking off … I really don't know how to handle that role (neutral chairman).
> If the teacher does stay as technician-librarian, in other words, there's the resource, get on with it.
> The teacher is acting as an observer.
> The teacher is to some extent merely a technician.
> The teacher is acting as a referee.
> The teacher has disappeared further into the background.

The sense of perplexity comes through clearly. Perhaps because of this perplexity it is not surprising that she viewed her low influence teaching negatively as words like 'merely' and 'just' suggest. Thus, the term 'technician' is probably used to suggest something less than a professional role for her. In low influence teaching she is cast as referee in a game whose purpose and rules are unclear.

How did she translate the vision into tradition? Let's look at how she handled the discussion lessons. In discussion lessons she was meant to discuss open-ended questions by exerting an indirect control of the process – how the discussion went on was more important than what was discussed. Students were expected to learn general problem-solving skills as a consequence of these discussions. She translated discussion lessons in a variety of ways. She treated the discussion material as a traditional teacher-directed lesson. When discussion questions came up, instruction was given where content mattered more than process. She did not know how to conduct the lesson according to the vision. She translated open-ended discussion material into end-of-chapter questions and had the students answer the questions as if they were the sort that could be answered by looking back in the chapter. Of course, no such answers could be found. None the less, this was better than risking the loss of influence that was associated with using an indirect approach.

She transferred a discussion lesson into an occasion for students to talk freely without any teacher guidance. Her comments suggested that she did not consider the discussion material serious. She saw the discussion episodes 'as pure waffle'. Compared to the certainty of the scientific content that she normally taught, discussion for her was a waste of time. Although she saw that the questions were meant to be discussed, she could not see that they led anywhere. A discussion was seen as pointless.

She used high influence teaching not only to keep students at their work and their behaviour within acceptable bounds, but also to obtain a sense that something was being accomplished, that work was being done.

Tradition and the uncertain role of the teacher

Role diffuseness

Wilson (1962) notes that teaching is a diffuse, diverse and difficult to delimit activity. One of the consequences of role diffuseness, he notes, is conflict and uncertainty. He lists six types of uncertainty that occur as a result of diffuseness. These uncertainties I see as dilemmas which, if uncontrolled, lead to uncertainty, confusion, and anxiety. However, they are controlled by teachers through translation of visions into traditional forms. They do this because they have to continue to function and to cope with uncertainty and thus they construe their practice to minimize the consequence of role diffuseness by intentionally resolving dilemmas in favour of tradition, one of whose functions is to delimit the work they do: to place it within manageable bounds. What are these dilemmas teachers face and how are they related to the process of translating visions into tradition?

Teachers face a dilemma associated with the loss of influence when they use the inquiry approach to science teaching which was part of the vision. They are urged to enter into a partnership with their students as they discuss science topics, but many science teachers do not know how to construe a discussion and instead search for familiar ways to deal with discussion-based investigations. None-too-successful 'hybrids' between what had been intended and what was familiar are common. These hybrids, I believe, are forms of adaptive response to proposals which alter authority relationships in the classroom. Inquiry-oriented teaching, when it occurs, undermines the social dimensions of influence. Teachers abandon the intellectual potentials of discussion (a major goal of the project) in order to maintain influence in the classroom, an influence bound up with being able to direct and edit effectively what happens in the classrooms.

The second dilemma concerns the absence of a clear line of demarcation whereby a teacher knows when the job the position demands has been done. Evidence of having done the job in teaching is not clear cut even at the best of times. Evidence of progress came from construing the accumulation of notebooks as 'making progress.' Information accumulated in notebooks fulfils a contract.

Since it was not clear what the visionary syllabus for the course was, considerable problems for the teachers emerged. A syllabus did not exist because the vision stressed thinking skills. However, teachers can not plan their work on the basis of teaching only skills. The more teachers stress how to think scientifically, the less they have to show for it. How do you point to progress in thinking in some material way?

The vision is based on an integrated approach to teaching, and teachers are faced with the prospect of teaching subject matter not familiar to them. Should they risk that or restructure the course along familiar lines? Again the dilemma is clear.

Teachers are subjected to complaints from parents who think that integrated subjects are not suitable to career objectives. Employers think the same. So do universities. Should teachers stand up for the project in spite of the complaints or should they see the project terminated? Either way there are unpleasant consequences.

Teachers are accused of not preparing acceptable candidates for advanced level science. It was said of them that they did not introduce the 'language' of the specialized disciplines. Thus chemists said their fellow chemists did not do a proper job. Should teachers persist with the visionary but inefficient project or should they re-establish smooth relations with their science department peers by a return to tradition? Should they recognize the concerns of their colleagues or affirm their commitment to the vision in spite of these unfavourable consequences? Dilemmas abound. Teachers, not visionaries, have to deal with them.

How do teachers maintain their role?

Teachers seek ways of assuring themselves and others that work is being done – they seek 'milestones' to remind them of their progress (National Science Foundation 1978). To change the metaphor, I would say that teachers have traditional, functioning ways of measuring the progress of the work of their classes and of their influence. Without a way of describing progress and measuring achievement, visions contain the seeds of their own demise. Their jargon comprehends neither the complex, stable systems in which the teachers operate, nor the subtle inter-connections between goals, expectations and techniques which protect at the expense of the practices urged by visions.

Dilemmas associated with visions are resolved at the expense of certain desirable goals. Problem solving and critical thinking are important visionary goals. Yet teachers see them in favour of more familiar goals and methods in order to protect them. How are we to view this? Are teachers doing the wrong thing?

We can imagine that the lack of a clearly defined syllabus creates significant problems for teachers in the classroom. The vision we have been considering had no such syllabus; only theoretical discussions of problem solving and critical thinking. However, teachers have to prepare pupils to pass internal and external examinations, and schools have elaborate techniques for accomplishing this based on the subject expertise of the teacher, clear and stable examination requirements, examination questions requiring recall, access to old examination questions, time to revise, completed student notebooks containing the material to be placed into memory, recitation, and, most importantly, trust on the part of students that what has been taught is factually accurate and relevant to what might be asked on the examination. Teachers possess expertise in operating this traditional system which engenders student confidence. Teachers take pride in this tradition. The syllabus establishes reasonable expectations for the teacher, indicating what is reliable information, and acting as the standard which guarantees the currency of teaching. Making sure pupils cover the syllabus is a limited goal to deal with. They do this in terms of content and officially can gloss the aims as they wish.

Teachers are concerned when there is a lack of a basis for assessing the progress of students. Students expect to have a basis upon which to revise and teachers look for some tangible measure of progress through the work. The dilemma is that developing problem-solving skills requires considerable classroom discussion of experimental results and of social issues related to science.

However, teachers must prepare their pupils for examinations. Students rely on the teacher and look for measures of their progress through the course. So, at the risk of minimizing the practice at problem solving, teachers isolate a syllabus of separate subjects and teach the course as if it were little different from the other examination courses. That meant stressing recall of information, not problem solving and critical thinking – but can one blame them for doing this?

The visionary project is not well adapted to these traditional functions. Preview is difficult, since subjects are submerged in the integrated format, and recruitment uncertain, since expectations about teachers, classrooms and subjects are not met. It is not surprising that some lobby against the vision because its organization and approved methods upset the functions so well supported by tradition.

An examination syllabus embodies the way specialized disciplines are to be understood in the school, and is used in connection with an effective tradition for passing on the information; it allows pupils to gain credentials. Teachers believe that pupils depend upon them for an interpretation of the point and direction of particular classroom events. Unless the teacher is there, the point is not going to be established.

Perrow (1965) has argued for the central role of know-how in the process of change. On the basis of his review of research into forms of therapy in mental hospitals, he noted that many mental hospitals seek 'economical custody' as a goal because there exists a body of know-how for custodial or housekeeping goals. Perrow suggests that 'social scientists have an unrealistic perception of the structure and goals of public mental hospitals because they fail to see how [know-how] influences the structure and goals' (p. 930).

Now there is a significant formal parallel between what innovators in mental care and science doctrine seek ('client centred therapy'/'new partnerships'), and what the institutions are able to provide ('custody at low cost'/ 'credentials'). This is not to equate the goals of the different institutions but only to show that in both cases goals are sought for which the needed know-how does not exist. Perrow goes on to show that the know-how also influences social relationships. In hospitals where economical custody is the care provided, matters such as who gets how much soap and other scarce resources are bones of contention between people. Similarly in schools, who obtains access to bright pupils, or whose students receive good examination marks or whose pupils are prepared for A Level are areas of contention. These status symbols are very much at issue in the way visionary projects are received in schools. What should visionaries do about this?

What visionaries fail to realize is that without the know-how that has to be there for the vision to succeed, teachers are not able to pursue the revised goals of the vision. Visionaries pay little attention to the practical matters of implementing their ideas. Materials directed at teachers are usually devoid of suggestions concerning the needed know-how. Teachers quite naturally continue to use traditional methods in the absence of anything better; it would be surprising if they did otherwise.

Documenting the work of teachers

What are teachers doing?

As Freire (1973) suggests, visionaries from outside the classroom must adopt a more humble role vis-à-vis those they wish to influence. The innovator may possess valid images of educational practice, but these images are nothing if they cannot be understood in terms of the functions of practice.

In the process of discussion between teacher educators and teachers, consideration of the implications for practice of the new procedures can act dialectically. Traditional – and perhaps long unexamined – practice can be challenged by new visions whose practical implications can be worked out with teachers; by trying these new ideas and discussing them with others, teachers can build the experiential base from which to develop a more powerful understanding of the functions and values of the existing traditions. The growth of this understanding is a dialectical process. New experience can show where tradition is inadequate and traditions can help teachers discuss the potential implications of the new visions. Innovators can begin to understand how their visions map onto the world of teachers – to see where there is a need for translation and where there are unrealistic assumptions. The new practice is thus carefully mapped onto the actual working lives of teachers – neither the adequacy of the new ideas, nor the inadequacy of the old are assumed. Dialectically each is used to assist the other.

A central consideration of the process is for both teacher and the outsider, innovator or educator to realize that they cannot automatically assume that each understands the other. Innovators have to understand the dilemmas that teachers face and why dilemmas are resolved as they are. Teachers need to understand the potential of the new ideas and assess their value. Such understanding has to be based on a knowledge of the particular circumstances in which the teachers work: the institutional realities and the sources of work satisfaction (for an extensive treatment of this issue see Reid, 1978).

The case of the translation of the science project into traditional practices suggests that how teachers construe their influence in the classroom has an important bearing on how particular innovative ideas will be adapted in use. The concept of influence needs to be probed further in order to understand how teachers see the link between tradition and the dilemmas of the practice of teaching. However, as we saw, much of what the teachers know is tacit – hidden behind a rhetorical facade not easily penetrated. Visionaries must meet with the teachers in such a way that the 'deep structure' of practice is revealed. Clinical methods such as those of Kelly have promise here if they are used heuristically and non-manipulatively. Teachers in the present study, for example, said that the clinical interviews had helped them probe their own thoughts, some of which they had not been aware of.

In getting below the surface the outsider holds the innovative idea tentatively. Those ideas are subject to an assessment of their practical implications in terms of an analysis of potential dilemmas. 'Governing variables' (Argyris and Schon 1974) that appear to control prevailing resolutions are analysed. The innovation thus acts as an heuristic device for probing value systems, instructional arrangements and classroom practice. Through this process new images of practice are revealed in a way that recognizes the complexities of practice itself and the difficulty of revealing and understanding how values, rationality, practice and context are connected.

Interpreting cases

Geertz (1973) argues that we must develop our theoretical understanding of human beings actively through the interpretation of cases as we have done in this chapter. He notes:

> Rather than beginning with a set of observations and attempting to subserve them under a governing law, [clinical inference] begins with a set of . . . signifiers and attempts to place them in an interchangeable frame . . . In the study of culture the signifiers are . . . clusters of symbolic acts and the aim is . . . the analysis of discourse.
>
> (Geertz 1973: 26)

He likens the work of the anthropologist to the work of clinical medicine or psychology. The theoretical work is directed towards the task of generating interpretation of matters already in hand but it must also be robust enough to allow us to understand new interpretive problems. How does case study allow us to generate such rich interpretive frameworks? How can the study of teaching advance through this kind of reflective analysis of cases we have been considering in this chapter? Let us consider this question in more detail.

Even if we have chosen educationally significant cases, what is to say our interpretation of them is justified? This is yet another way of raising questions about validity. Dray (1957) provides useful advice in his discussion of this issue. We have already considered the matter of significance (what he calls the *pragmatic* test of validity). He suggests that another test be applied to our cases as a way of further assessing their validity.

The reason for the behaviour must be something under human control; so that either something done or undone could matter in the kind of case being written. There is an essential link between assigning responsibility to agents and attributing casual status. Dray (1957) says that: 'unless we are prepared to hold the agent responsible for what happened, we cannot say his action was a cause'. This test is called the *inductive* test of validity; it assures us that there is some justification for singling out the reasons we have.

Beyond the issue of validity there is a matter of the generality of the case findings. Dray (1957) notes, for example, that in many case studies of accidents excessive speed has been implicated as a cause. Although excessive speed cannot be predicted to be a cause in advance based on covering laws, it is a likely potential cause of an accident. Given the frequency with which excessive speed is a factor in accidents we can generalize about the place of excessive speed in accidents. It is on this kind of basis that we can accumulate knowledge through case study.

How might we apply this idea to cases involving teaching? Again, I would like to use a personal example. We saw above that in order to understand the way the teachers have construed the relationship between teaching and the curriculum, we have had to look at the 'expressive' dimension (Harre 1979) of their behaviour; that is at what they are saying about themselves as teachers through their teaching behaviour. Argyris and Schon (1974) call these purposes 'governing variables', and, like them, it is particularly those affective dimensions of teaching such as control of anxiety, self-esteem, and other aspects of the presentation of self that seem very much at issue in understanding the fate of innovations in classrooms. We have seen in this chapter how these governing variables work in traditional teaching.

We have seen that teachers are concerned with being 'modern', with being effective guides to the 'system', with being good at selecting and 'editing' material which will be externally examined, with being quick to unravel classroom problems, with being 'on track', and so on.

But what hinges on this sort of general knowledge about teaching? I argue that such knowledge can be the basis for a more effective practice. Normally research on teaching focuses on instrumental matters: gain scores; teacher and student attributes of one kind or another; or personality measures. However, I want to claim that certain kinds of expressive purposes are heavily implicated in understanding how teachers enact the curriculum; and how they affect their students. We cannot predict teacher behaviour on the basis of our understanding of these expressive issues in teaching, but we now know to look for them when writing our cases in order to understand what causes it.

Without knowledge of past practice in particular cases, we have no way of understanding what might happen in the future if people were to try to change their teaching approach. Cases tell us about why people do what they do and why they persist in doing it. Collingwood (1946) characterized case study as a way of 'knowing ourselves'. As we become the subject of case study an opportunity for self-knowledge is created through the critical interpretation of our actions by another, and through that to critical self-interpretation to autobiography.

Such a practice lies at the heart of Argyris and Schon's (1974) approach to professional self-education, for example. Their method asks individuals to subject experience to a reflective analysis to find out why they do what they do. Based on many cases of professional behaviour, Argyris and Schon have concluded that much of professional behaviour is systematically sealed off from critical appraisal. The status of this claim, by the way, is no different from Dray's 'speed kills' or my look for the expressive aspects of teaching when explaining the fate of innovations.

The researcher and the teacher

How do reflective studies contribute to opening up behaviour for critical study? The study of one's own practice is subject to one's own critical analysis as well as that of the researcher. Researchers are contemporaries and share an understanding of the events at hand which are given significance in terms of the setting. The relevant features of this setting and its boundaries are open for discussion. Neither teacher nor researcher alone can isolate episodes for case study because each is conditioned and shaped by some significant problem of his/her own which depends on what educational issues are taken to be important.

The past we wish to study is recent and the testimony is live. We can talk to the person whose case we are considering. This gives our contemporary case studies an additional resource, because we researchers can probe the testimony directly and we can control how the testimony is obtained; we can ask for comments on it and we can get behind it. Our inquiries are not limited to considering the behaviour of teachers in terms of their purposes, but they cannot avoid those purposes.

There is yet a further educational potential of reflection on cases. Teachers do things for reasons they are not always aware of. They are subject to social pressures and constraining forces with which they cope, but on a relatively unconscious basis. It is here that cases become subject to analysis in terms of social forces and unconscious causes, but not to the extent of saying that the teacher has no part in his or her behaviour; only that the behaviour is relatively less controlled by conscious processes and relatively difficult to construe. Having made every effort to understand the teacher's behaviour in terms of purposes, we might want to consider the forces which shape the context in which teachers act.

As researchers, we are interested in why people really did what they did, but they may not know very well why they did what they did; sometimes what they did seems not to be in their interest. What are we to make of this? In this regard, Theodore Mischel's (1964) analysis of the logic of clinical activity is helpful. He suggests that the researcher try to construe relatively unconscious motives as reasons for action as a basis for making apparently odd behaviour seem less odd. In terms of these odd intentions the researcher can construct a 'calculation' which shows that seen from the person's point of view, apparently odd behaviour would seem justified; would seem the right or appropriate thing to do, and the person can, at least ideally, be helped to see that he/she has really been operating in terms of a rationale whose nature is hidden. In other words, we should do everything possible to see how behaviour might make sense from the agent's point of view even though the agent is relatively unconscious of it. Difficult to understand actions can be understood in the same way as more easily understandable actions. This is a critical point to consider when writing case studies. Of course there are limits to this. Let me illustrate this point by again citing an actual case.

To return to the case we discussed above of Ms Markle using discussion in her science classroom, we saw that in most cases traditional classroom routines did not work well, yet she persisted with the innovative course. She was reluctant to give it up. At first we could not understand this. We found it odd that she was willing to persist with what looked to us flawed teaching strategies. With probing we found that she wanted her students to enjoy up-to-date approaches to the subject. The difficulties were worth enduring, it seems, because she enjoyed the status of being involved in a modern science project. She saw her work with the project as a way of being 'modern' – of expressing something about the kind of teacher she is. This perception, which overruled the concern about classroom routines which did not work at all well, allowed her to claim that her students and the school were involved in the new ways of teaching science.

Our understanding of the way she construes the impact of new curricula in her classrooms is that she values participation in new projects as a symbol to be used *expressively* (Harre 1979) to enhance her standing in the eyes of students, parents and principal. The *instrumental* outcomes – gaining credentials or insight into subjects – could be ignored at least at the outset since they were not immediately part of the expressive process. In the end, of course, expressive and instrumental purposes are linked, and as she works her way through the expressive dimensions of her task, it is likely that instrumental issues will receive more attention, as they did, in the end. How quickly the process occurs and how it might be facilitated are important further questions for reflection.

I do not want to suggest here that often teachers do odd things – only that at times we may not understand their behaviour, and that teachers may not be aware immediately of the reasons why they act as they do, or not aware of all of the reasons. Thus examining their behaviour is a complex process of reconstructing as fully as possible their real reasons for doing what they are doing; of rendering their behaviour as intelligible. Thus their cases become a basis for critical reflection as we and they engage in an evaluation of them. What looked to us 'odd' behaviour became understandable in the light of the purposes of the teachers we believe we have uncovered. Of course the further question remains: are these purposes justifiable? That is yet another issue to which an examination of cases gives rise to. Another question also remains. What if a calculation for the teachers' behaviour cannot be rendered? Here we have to look for causes beyond the reasons of the teacher, and we enter the domain of pathology.

Not all high grade actions are performed deliberately in the sense that they are undertaken with a plan consciously formulated (Ryle 1949; Polanyi 1958). Whatever the level of conscious deliberation, there is an account which can be constructed for it and it is by producing some such account that we explain by showing how action and intention are linked. To do this we have to attend to the expressive and instrumental aspects of actions and intentions.

For teachers to understand their own actions after the event, they have to construct an account even though at the time of the action no such account was in their mind. Even so, not any account will do. As Dray (1957) says, 'when we do consider ourselves justified in accepting an explanation of an individual action it will most often assume the general form of an agent's [account]'. We are not going to be especially satisfied with an account that the teacher doesn't recognize. The researcher must probe behind the initial construction of events to see if there are any motives that have not been articulated. Since the subject of our case is alive we can do that. Dray points out that we may have to accept some odd principles of action, and we may not agree with these and yet be able to see the rationale from the person's point of view.

The danger is that research which begins as an *explanation* of teacher behaviour can easily end up by being an *evaluation* of it in relation to certain norms of a model prescribing what information teachers ought to think about and how their minds ought to process that information. It is not surprising that teachers have failed to live up to these norms.

It is also a mistake to concentrate only on what teachers *say* about what they are doing. Just as loudly do their actions speak about what they are doing, and it is often the case that what people espouse concerning action and what they 'say' *in* action are different (Argyris and Schon 1974). In the end we are interested in how teachers teach, that is in how they act in their classrooms, and in understanding why they act this way. However, this does not mean that we are not interested in how teachers talk about what they do.

Accumulating views that people have about their work helps us appreciate the range of perspectives they bring to that work; yet one doesn't only want to know *what* people think, one wants also to understand *why* they approach problems in the way they do. We want to explain their behaviour in classrooms. As a student of teaching, one's puzzle is that teachers don't seem to solve problems according to official norms; or even as they say *they* would act. Indeed, there seems to exist a wide variety of ideas among teachers about how these problems can be solved, but these ideas are expressed or not expressed in practice itself; that is the key point.

Why did this or that teacher solve this or that problem as he or she did? To understand that, we have to understand how the teacher solved the problem, and once we can work the teachers' calculation metaphorically and literally we can understand why the teacher tried to solve it in such a way. We have to engage in critical reflection with that teacher, and having done that, there may be common features in the accounts that teachers give of their approach to these problems from which we can generalize, and features of their thinking which might alert us to look for this or that element in the beginning phase of our subsequent case studies.

From the kind of studies we have been discussing can come a body of general knowledge which can be shared; which can become the basis of an increasingly sophisticated awareness on the part of *researchers* of what to look for in their study of teachers, on the part of *policy* makers as they commission and interpret research and, most importantly, on the part of the *teacher* as he/she engages with these others in considering practice. This is the hope for critical reflection on teaching.

5

What it takes to take teaching seriously

Change as a process of dialogue

There has been no lack of innovative ideas to guide school practices. Periodically, large sums of money are spent on this subject or that; most often on mathematics and science as the nation is seen to be at risk because not enough people take these subjects. Teachers are exhorted to change their practice: often these changes are radical – so radical that teachers do not change. Why should they? Important purposes are tied up in how they teach now, the results of a complex negotiation amongst teachers, pupils and others about what is worth studying and how it can best be done in the classroom.

How things got the way they are must be understood. So must what these ways signify about important but often tacitly held values. As we saw in earlier chapters teachers act out what they know rather than put that knowing into words. The acting out has to be interpreted and so does the interpretation itself. Such a process presupposes a community of teachers concerned to do worthwhile things in schools – they speak the same 'language' about events whose significance is commonly understood. Usually they do. Times change and practices and their purposes part company: routines become rituals and bad 'deals' are made with politicians and bureaucrats to shape the work of the school to their purposes. Practices may degenerate under pressure of time and lack of resources and energy. Students change; political realities change; the family changes. Well-established practices have to be reviewed. A running dialogue between what is said through practice and what wants saying must be maintained. How are we to think of such dialogue? That is one element of the interpretive process to be considered in this chapter. What does it take to enter successfully into such a dialogue? That is another question we have to consider in thinking about an interpretive approach to change.

Innovations like computers are important because they ask teachers to confront their routine approaches to teaching: to make sense of them and thus become more aware of the value of what they do. Professional development happens when the value of practice is re-appraised. There is more at stake for teachers than learning to master new routines when they adopt innovative approaches to learning. The importance of existing topics and methods are considered in the light of the potential of innovations. We have to appreciate why we do things the way we do.

As Vickers (1970) points out:

> The appreciated world is selected by our interests; for only some interest would lead us to notice any of its constituents. Of course, we have many contexts which we fail to notice . . . These neglected relations force themselves on our attention in time and thus become part of our appreciated world. This appreciated world, thus limited, is given form by our expectations. For it is these which, matching or not-matching the unrolling stream of events, confirm or call it into question . . . They reassure us that an appreciated world is sufficiently in accord with the real world to be serviceable . . . Our appreciated world is given meaning by our standards of judgement, ethical, aesthetic, political and other . . . I thus conceive our appreciated world as carved out by our interests, structured by our expectations and evaluated by our standards of judgement.
>
> (Vickers 1970: 98)

Interpretation – what Vicker's calls appreciation – is a way of knowing much more about the meaning of existing practices in schools – about the way teachers make sense of their work. Professional development, as we discussed in an earlier chapter, is not just a matter of teachers developing enhanced cognitive capacities – of being more expert – it is also a question of coming to know their culture in more productive ways. Unfortunately this is not the way professional development is thought of in educational systems. If we look at currently dominant conceptions we find that reflection on practice is not central.

The approach to change that now dominates the theory and practice of professional development is the systems model that we discussed in chapter one: inputs (decisions) and outputs (what happens in the classroom) are intended to be coupled. The parts of the system are arranged to ensure that central directives will be implemented – that people will act according to system plans, and that if they do not, the nature of the system is adjusted to improve the link between inputs and outputs. In the process, teachers are assigned practices to implement which supplant what they are already doing

– often this requires them to break with practices which have a long history. We have seen above the difficulties that can lead to.

Reflecting on practice in its cultural context is central to the interpretive process. Teachers do act rationally to solve effectively problems that confront them but they are not always conscious of how they do these things and not able to put their know-how easily into words, as we saw. Improvement begins when teachers confront the meaning of their practice.

We have to focus on the *meaning* of practice when we think about changing it. Teaching is an activity in which, as we have seen, teachers express things about themselves, about school subjects and about their relationships to students through their teaching. We saw examples of this process in earlier chapters.

Changing a practice isn't merely a technical process – it involves considering what the change signifies. That entails dialogue – a conversation between the old and the new. Some, those who hold a technocentric view of change, say that such a dialogue is futile because innovations involve technical matters that practitioners cannot understand. This is a fake idea.

Change involves values as well as technical issues. It isn't sufficient to be *au courant* with the latest scientific theories underlying the change ideas, to be the change agent or expert: values inherent in the old and the new practices are at issue. The old is not to be discarded out of hand. The significance of change must be considered. This requires dialogue.

Through such dialogue among practitioners and between them and innovators the significance of practice can develop but only if the ethos of the practitioner is understood. Freire (1973) cites change in agricultural practices as an example of the importance of appreciating the ethos of the practitioners:

> To discuss erosion ... [it] must appear to the peasants in their 'basic' view as a real problem, and as a 'distinct perception' firmly related to other problems. Erosion is not merely a natural problem ... taking it as a challenge is cultural.
>
> (Freire 1973: 109)

Dialogue enables outsiders and insiders to probe the meaning of practice – to see what it signifies. Dialogue also enables practitioners to see conflicts amongst theories which guide their action and become aware that they may not always do what they ought to do. These conflicts often lie unrecognized because people avoid confronting them. Such conflicts can become productive 'dilemmas' when they strike at matters of central concern to the person. As Argyris and Schon (1974) suggest:

> The [practitioner] strives to be effective and to keep constant his theory-in-use and the behavioural world he has created. When finally he cannot do both in spite of his full repertoire of defence, he may change the

governing variables of his theory-in-use. This dialogue shapes the theory building process.

(Argyris and Schon 1974: 34)

The dialogue uncovers the values which underlie practice and are often not surfaced. With these values in view the practitioner can re-assess and re-align practice to more closely relate it to fundamental values. This dialogue takes place against a background of actual working conditions – against the culture of the classroom.

In this interpretive process practitioners and outsiders collaborate in revealing what the practice says and assessing that against a backdrop of educational values. Outsiders cannot participate in this process unless they understand the culture in which the existing practice takes place. Profound cultural understanding is absolutely indispensable for effective collaboration (Freire 1973).

Take the example of the architect, which Argyris and Schon (1974) point to, to illustrate the process of interpretation and the central role of dialogue in it:

The architect's effective performance will depend on his ability to immerse himself in a network of behavioural worlds – the architect's ability to get inside these worlds and comprehend their culture will affect his execution of the project.

(Argyris and Schon 1974: 158)

Outsiders must be able to enter into the world in which buildings will live. Buildings say things. What they are to say depends on what matters in the world where they will be:

Like the anthropological visitor to a culture, the architect must see which pieces of information are central and which are peripheral; he [or she] must attempt to see the perspective of those he encounters. And he [or she] must somehow construct for himself their way of looking at the world.

(Argyris and Schon 1974: 159)

Like buildings, agricultural practices exist in a web of significance. Agricultural practices cannot be treated as mere technical problems:

Erosion, reforestation, seed time or harvest have a relation to peasant attitudes, to religion, to the cult of the dead, to the illnesses of animals. All these aspects are contained within a cultural totality. As a structure this cultural totality reacts as a whole ... It is thus not possible for the agronomist-educator to attempt to change these attitudes ... unless she/he is familiar with the peasants' view of the world and unless she/he takes it as a whole.

(Freire 1973: 108–9)

There are, of course, barriers to achieving dialogue. They may be due to
the way people have to live their lives – to the kind of institutions in which
lives are led – in Freire's case absentee landlords (latifundists) control
the land and deny participation in decision-making to the peasants. These
peasants accept that this is their role – that it is the way things are.
This view of themselves is a major barrier to critical dialogue. Dialogue
itself is one way to begin to examine the nature of the social system which
underlies practice. Dialogue is a way of beginning to reform the very
structure of action so that it can better support the critical goals of the dialogical process. It is not hard to see how these examples can be applied to
education.

Institutions erect barriers to dialogue through belief that practices can be
controlled by techniques based on laws discovered by social science. Such
beliefs are characterized by 'standardized and measurable components, control through measurement of output and capacity for controlled variation'
(Argyris and Schon 1974: 152). Such environments create a behavioural world
in which people have 'A low sense of effectiveness, self-worth and vitality
and learning ... [such a world] is not conducive to cumulative personal
development' (p. 154).

Professionals who work in institutions committed to scientism are cut off
from the liberating possibilities of reflection. Belief in technical solutions
rule out forms of human interaction which might reveal dysfunction and
might yield better practices. Fear of losing control, of appearing doubtful, of
not winning, dominate. Instead of critical dialogue those who own and
depend on the techniques 'sell' them. Dialogue about the old and the new
is not part of the agenda – being successful at selling the new is. Such a
process has not been successful in education. Not understanding the culture
of teachers, innovators typically receive only superficial acceptance as the
literature on change amply demonstrates.

Understanding the tension between the old and the new

The old and the new

The tension between the old and the new is the engine which drives critical
reflection – it is the source of energy for interpretation. The new always says
something about the old – often the new is seen as a criticism of the old.
The new, wherever it comes from, causes reflection about the old – it introduces new language, upsets old assumptions, threatens loss and promises
plenty. What can be made of this critical tension for professional
development?

Let us think of the impact of computers on classrooms as an example of
the new. There is little newer than computers in schools. But computers have

to be installed in schools – literally – and they have to find their way into the language of educational practice. Computers are novel and they challenge the routine. They can stand as an example of the new. How does this tension reveal itself? Let us look in detail at how teachers 'adopt' computers:

> Procedures required to launch and sustain drill and practice activity at the computer do not appear to strain existing routines too far, but having to support computer activity parallel to teaching the rest of the class does place strain on the teacher. Logo requires novel responses and does not fit in with familiar teaching routines . . . Adapting elements of innovation to familiar routines is an important issue [for] teachers [who] cannot be expected to suddenly abandon their practice in favour of teaching activities quite remote from what they are used to. The experience of innovation cannot be all novelty. There is simply too much at stake, and yet a totally routine approach to innovation is no innovation at all. There has to be enough that is novel to pose a challenge to practice.
>
> However, the process is not one of substituting one practice for another but of subjecting existing practices to a challenge posed by another well-conceived practice. The effect of the challenge is to provide reasons to modify the existing practice through a process of critical comparison.
>
> (Olson and Eaton 1987: 189–90)

A good example of such adaptation can be seen in the way teachers launched educational computing as a new elementary school subject:

> Rather than establishing a time when all students would study this subject (and thereby render the one machine useless), the teachers adopted a rota system. Access to the computer was incorporated into the rewards and punishment structure of the classroom. Teachers are used to doing more than one thing at once by setting the students work that 'runs itself'. They used this strategy with the computer as far as they could . . . [Students] required much more support than was expected, and this created problems for the 'run itself' approach to the subject. . . .
>
> Another novel aspect of using computers for instruction was the ambiguity of student problems at the computer. Were they due to machine, software, or student characteristics? The extra demand on teachers that resulted from having to sort out delay and interruption episodes was a novel aspect of using computers and one not easily handled by existing routines.
>
> (Olson and Eaton 1987: 190)

What is going on here? The computer calls into question the very way teachers think about their usefulness to students. First, teachers are no longer confident that they can be helpful – too many students require too much of their time. And even if they had the time to give they are not sure just what help is wanted. The whole basis of teacher efficacy is called into question. This is no mean challenge. What are teachers to make of such a challenge?

Innovation means teachers have to work harder and they are likely to ask, is the work worth it? This is not a matter of a mercenary quid pro quo. Teachers are rational people given to the pursuit of their best interests like the rest of us. They want to put the best face on their practice. In the process of dialogue the value of their work is assessed, as is the relative importance of different benefits from innovation. Some of these benefits are quite tangible. They help teachers do the work: they smooth the way, or not. But other benefits – and drawbacks – are more profound. As we saw above, they call into question the very values which are embedded in the everyday practices of the teacher.

> A useful way of thinking about how teachers respond to innovation is to look at *instrumental* and *expressive* elements of their behaviour ... Instrumental behaviour is directed at producing student learning. Expressive behaviour is directed at creating respect for the teacher and liking for the subject, for example. This expressive behaviour can have an indirect effect on learning by creating an appropriate climate, and learning outcomes may come to influence how expressive behaviour is appraised. A given teaching behaviour has both expressive and instrumental elements in varying degrees. [Table 6 gives examples of instrumental and expressive aspects of educational computing].
>
> The usefulness of this distinction lies in the fact that, without it, it is difficult to make sense of a variety of teacher decisions. Indeed, without it, teacher decisions can seem contradictory and confused. How is one to make sense of the idea that a teacher does not favour Logo as a way of learning programming yet is quite happy for students to tutor each other in Logo, or that a teacher wants to continue an experiment that she considers impossible to do?
>
> From an instrumental point of view, for reasons we have discussed, teaching the class how to program through Logo is not favoured but, from an expressive point of view, it is seen as allowing enthusiastic students the opportunity to experience a challenge. In his own eyes, and hopefully in theirs, the teacher is someone who appreciates the needs of some children for self-directed computer activity in spite of the fact that he does not consider Logo useful. But instrumental issues are not at issue here. By allowing students to explore Logo the teacher expresses his interest in computer-literate students and displays his willingness to let them teach themselves. In this way he maintains certain important relationships with these children ...
>
> Do these expressive 'statements' matter? We think that they do

because they are part of the kind of social person a teacher is, part of the way teachers make statements about what matters to them and what sort of climate for learning they are trying to create. The way they view their accomplishments as teachers is in no small way related to these personal statements, and it is important for teachers to recognize what they mean.

Innovations often involve new ways of assigning meaning to practice. Teaching something using the computer means something different in expressive terms from teaching the same material some other way. Teachers are aware of these meanings and their significance, and are engaged in a process of re-assigning meanings as they try new practices. Making these processes more explicit is a way of learning from the process of innovation and could be a valuable part of in-service education as teachers systematically analyse the pay-off they sought in teaching about computers.

(Olson and Eaton 1987: 191–2)

How can we use the tension of the old and the new, the instrumental and the expressive, to interpret teaching? Where does dialogue amongst people lead who are prepared to see what their practice says and to critically assess what they are saying?

Steps towards interpretation

Recovering the significance of practice is a key step in launching a dialogue about the old and the new. In order to illustrate how this recovery process works I want again to take an example from our research on computers. It is clear that access to computers is something students eagerly want. Teachers realize this. Teachers we talked to have used computers as part of the reward structure of the school. The old and the new have found a compatible way of getting on together. Or have they? Let us see what happens when innovation meets tradition. Consider the following case.

Case Study 5: Rewards in Mr Shaw's classroom

We found that Mr Shaw used the computer to reward certain children who behaved well. Students who assiduously did their work were allowed to go to the computer when their turn came up, but those who had not worked lost their turn. What was he up to? He controlled the students through computer access. The computer acted as a familiar use of reward tokens. This is one part of the story. There is more than meets the eye.

What is Mr Shaw saying to the class about their collective life? What is he saying about computers? This dimension of practice – the expressive – is often ignored when we reflect on practice. What if Mr Shaw reflected on the expressive part of his classroom life?

Often there is no reason to reflect on classroom life because practice is taken for granted. But innovations which highlight new ways of doing things cause an occasion for reflection on the well-established routines. The new practices call into question what has become well established. The reward structure in Mr Shaw's classroom may remain unexamined until something like the computer brings it into focus. As others have found, microcomputers do challenge the reward structure of the classroom. The advent of the computer brings more than new tokens – it brings questions about token giving itself (Brine 1983).

In our example we can see how such a question might emerge. Certain students are rewarded very well. These students – called computer whizzes – are allowed to help other students, and to do this often move very freely about the classroom. Rather than work on tasks assigned to the rest of the class, the whizzes are allowed to help other students using computers. Some students have always been allowed special privileges, but the computer whizzes seem to have freedoms that go beyond monitors and helpers. They have special knowledge of computers which Mr Shaw does not have. This arcane knowledge gains for them a licence to wander the classroom and not do the tasks the rest have to do.

We can use a simple matrix to summarize our thoughts about how teachers use computers to reward students (Table 6). What seemed everyday [*routine*] – what seemed unusual [*novel*]? How did they accomplish their intentions [*instrumental actions*]? What lay behind the methods they adopted? What were they really saying about what they valued in their classrooms [*expressive actions*]?

Using the matrix we can begin to ask critical questions about the reward process in Mr Shaw's classroom as it is affected by innovation. These questions suggest how professional growth can emerge from interpreting the routine and novel and the instrumental and expressive elements of practice. Let us use the matrix to probe further the question of reward in the classroom.

Computer experts at liberty to move about the class on special missions

Table 6   An analysis of the computer as a reward

	Instrumental	*Expressive*
Routine	if you do your work you get computer time	computer time is valuable and scarce (is computer time so valuable?)
Novel	if you are a computer expert you don't have to do ordinary tasks	relieving the teacher is more important than doing certain tasks (ought teachers to liberate students from school tasks this way?)

where they may know more than Mr Shaw are novel. What does the novelty mean? How is the novel relationship related to other similar, but routine relationships and what they mean? What new teacher-student relationships and new reward patterns do these computer experts portend?

Mr Shaw has extended the idea of reward from the usual 'you can do this if you do that' to something more complex – certain students can now play novel roles in his classroom – they are rewarded in novel ways. Changes have occurred in traditional teacher-student relationships. The shift from routine to novel is one way of looking at growth which occurs as Mr Shaw reflects on the meaning of these changes.

These are questions for critical reflection which might allow him to probe the meaning for his practice in relation to the innovation with which he is experimenting. It is through this kind of reflection that teacher development can occur – teacher development aimed at the enhanced capacity to understand one's own practice.

Critically interpreting practice

This view of 'development' is not the same as, say, training teachers to implement this or that plan made elsewhere. Indeed it could be argued that the latter view of development is in fact anti-development in so far as teachers simply are asked to abandon what they do and take up something else – such a process hardly can be called development.

Professional development occurs when teachers move between thinking about the practical consequences of instrumental actions and thinking about the moral implications of expressive actions. At the instrumental level, the teacher considers how to accomplish the tasks of the classroom, but at the expressive level the teacher considers what those ways of doing things mean and what their value really is – what they say about the values of the teacher. In this way the ideas of everyday and novel practice can be analysed. Teachers can become more aware and critical of how they teach, of what the new method offers and, fundamentally, of what they value. This recovery and analysis of the meaning of the old and the new practices, and the dialogue between them, is how change becomes a true process of professional growth – a process of real teacher development. We can see how such a process can work by examining in detail the case of a teacher caught up in the process of school improvement through increased use of information technology.

Being willing to critically reflect on one's teaching is asking much of teachers. Teachers are not alone in this – it is a collective responsibility because teaching is a community affair with a moral purpose. What do I mean by this, you might well ask. Let us look more closely at the moral basis of the work of teachers. To do this I again want to use an example from our research as a case in point. It illustrates in much more detail the kind of analysis we explored above in the case of reward tokens in the classroom. This time we will consider reward tokens that are offered to teachers. It is the same reward, as you may have guessed – access to computers. Our examination – our interpretation – of the story will lead us to consider what it takes to take teaching seriously, which is the theme of this chapter.

Case Study 6: Ms Abt's avante-garde classroom

Ms Abt is an avant-garde teacher of English who is very interested in modern approaches to her subject. She has tried out a recent innovation in writing involving multiple drafts and student to student conferencing.

She has been given a computer by her school system to study the writing process which now involves word processing. Through student to student conferences, re-drafting to improve writing, and access to computers to encourage these activities, she thinks writing might improve. She has chosen 'treatment' and control groups in line with the approved research method- ology of the school board. The 'treatment' group of students are given extra time at the computer and extra attention from her:

> I say to [the students]: 'How would you like to work on the computer a little more often than perhaps some of the other students? You'll be part of a group of ten kids who are going to work until about March. You will have to write a little bit more but the pay-off will be that you will have a little bit more time on the computer.
>
> I want to find out if word processing contributes to better writing. One of the advantages of word processing on the computer is being able to move material around ... Access to the machine motivates the students and gives them a sense that they're on their own.

The practice is avant-garde. Student to student conferencing and creating multiple drafts of writing are novel. In order to 'amplify' her avant-garde, novel practice she ties it to the computer.

Ms Abt convinced the school board she would do something 'research-like' and 'psychological' with her computer. She got the computer by acceding to a particular way of looking at practice which emphasizes collection of data about the *instrumental* efficiency of the microcomputer:

> You know you're looking at slight changes in the group. It will be interesting to see how, not just the superficial types of revisions in terms of spelling corrections or the conventions [change]. You can hopefully try to raise their level of thinking, because they have to conference with two other students at least and then at least once with me.

She thinks she is expected to do experimental research to (the horse race study) within a formal view of the object of her research ('levels of thinking').

She is looking to see if the computer enhances generic process skills much favoured amongst the educational theorists who influence the school system. She says she will gather hard objective data about the efficiency of the computer as an aid to writing.

She is not encouraged to consider expressive matters. She attends to form at the expense of substance. She did not ask for a printer and a second disk drive both of which make it easier for students to use the word processing software. She emphasizes cognitive skills rather than good writing.

Now we should be clear in her defence. She is not the author of this instrumental approach. She uses it to get a computer and to pursue her avant-garde interests. But an experimental design means that only certain students are given extra attention – one computer allows no more. Students who volunteer, who do not include less able students, receive extra teacher attention and extra computer time in return for co-operating in the research.

What about the evident question of fairness? Is this part of the research? No, it is not. The experimental nature of the project justifies this apparent inequitable distribution of resources, Ms Abt believes. What actually happens?

Sally, one of the students not granted extra access, is disappointed because her print-out of a geometric poem she had constructed on the screen did not conform to what was on her screen. Sally has to struggle on on her own. Sally is a student with learning difficulties who deserved extra attention as much as the project students did. Ought Sally to be given what the other students were given?

Mark wants to keep his work private but is treated as a rogue. Privacy is an important issue in the use of microcomputers. Is this question part of the research? No, it is not.

These basic moral questions are not part of Ms Abt's research agenda. That agenda does not encourage her to ask these questions. A 'Faustian bargain' has been struck – she gains access to a scarce resource and the board distributes resources in a superficially even-handed way while maintaining a rational research-like posture aimed at documenting the efficiency of the computer and the efficiency of computer-based learning.

Questions about the effect of computers on classroom life are not asked. Is there fairness in distributing computer access? What purposes do computers have? Only efficiency is at issue. Why might any of us want to make such a bargain and what makes it Faustian? We have to leave this story at this point and find a way of making sense of it.

To do this we need to look closely at the expressive dimension of practice – at what is being said through practice (Geertz 1983). Practice is, after all, a social process and if we are to understand the nature of the practice we have to enter the imaginative universe of the teacher. What are Ms Abt and the other teachers we talked to – she was not alone – up to?

A critical interpretation

What would lead Ms Abt and other teachers to persist with what looked to us – and at times to her and the others, upon reflection – as an unrewarding technology? One clue lay in what she was doing before she took up with computers. When we examine how she taught before she had a computer we find she was already interested in novel approaches to writing. Her practice was already avant-garde. Why, then, move to computers?

Ms Abt obtained a powerful symbol for communicating her interest in innovative methods to university people to show how efficient computers were and thus justify their expense. To compete for a scarce resource, and to draw attention to her avant-gardism, she used the computer as a way to 'speak' about what she valued. She used a culturally approved symbol to signal her avant-gardism – the computer becomes a megaphone.

However, the very capacity of this technology to express commitment to and amplify new practices, while its greatest strength, is also the source of its seductive power. New technologies, being rewards in themselves and keys to further rewards, tempt all of us to pursue ends other than those which give our practice worth. MacIntyre (1984) calls such goods 'external' to practice:

> It is characteristic of … external goods that when achieved they are always some individual's property or possession … [T]he more some-one has of them, the less there is for other people. This is sometimes necessarily the case, as with power and fame … External goods are … objects of competition. It is characteristic of [internal goods] that their achievement is a good for the whole community who participate in the practice.
>
> (MacIntyre 1984: 190–91)

What was seductive about the new technology? Gaining access to it provides Ms Abt with a tool with which she could signal her avant-gardism. But are these technologies helping her practice better? Are these technologies worth competing for? Is it worth joining the cult of efficiency in order to get a computer? Does she pay a high price to get hold of such a symbol?

Take the process of getting the computer. The pilot project application form asked teachers to do research-like activities in order to produce data useful to the school system. They were to see if, by using computers as a treatment, certain gains could be measured. The framework assumed that teaching technique was at issue, practice was uniform across levels of schooling, and that appraisal of computers in classrooms was a technical problem. Teachers thus were required to orient their projects to the political demands (external goods) of the institution for hard data about the efficiency of computer-assisted learning rather than to pursue the moral implications that emerged out of practice itself (internal goods), and to consider the value of the new technology in the light of their experience.

The competitive framework in which the pilot projects were run is not, however, of the teacher's making. It is root and branch a part of the cult of efficiency of the institution in which they work.

The institutional process of giving access to scarce but desirable rewards in the name of efficiency and asking for something politically useful in sustaining the efficiency approach makes it harder for practitioners to do what ought to be done – reflect on the value of the new practices. Had Ms Abt been encouraged to reflect on the value of her computer use, her capacity to learn from the experience of change would have increased. What is required of her in order to counter the cult of efficiency? It takes virtue because the pressures for efficiency are great.

What policies would be needed to foster a critical approach to professional development? Change is a process of dialogue in which old and new practices speak to each other. There has to be respect for existing practice, parity amongst the players, and humility and awareness of the values of existing practice and of the defects of the new processes. The change of practice is not something that can be accomplished through the mandates of bureaucracy. But here there is the danger. Teacher development, as I see it, often is a thinly disguised process of teacher manipulation.

Our thinking about computers in education, to return to that example, has to take this holistic view. If the promise of computers is to be fulfilled, teachers must be able to use computers in forms of teaching which, although often difficult, are well within the scope of what they already know how to do. Helping students interpret experience, for example, is part of what teachers have always done. The computer permits a much richer exploration of experience and demands a high level of competence on the part of the teacher so that students might fully benefit from computer-based learning. Experience with computers challenges teachers to reappraise the way they deal with the experience of students. In doing this they have to think again about how they exert influence in their classroom as we have seen in the example above of classroom reward.

Critical reflection in practice

How is such an approach to change to work in practice? First, and crucially, teachers would need to sample their practice – audio or videotape it, or write journals about it and thus begin to see what is novel and routine and to see what these elements of practice mean. Such a process of recovering the nature of one's practice requires examples of the way one teaches – a reflection on how one works. The teacher might also consult students or colleagues – indeed, one might ask consultants to help.

For their part, innovators and consultants would need to be clear about what ideas about classroom practice are embodied in their thinking.

Much more care would have to be given to writing teacher guides which explained the assumptions of the innovation – the idea of innovation needs to be expressed clearly. A dialogue needs to be established instead of compliance.

Teachers may need help to recover the significance of their practice and see what new ideas imply for further action. Because such analysis and critique requires a high level of skills analysis, teachers might want to pursue further study to acquire these skills. Releasing teachers to take Master's degrees in education might be appropriate, and as part of in-service education, third parties could help teachers recover these ideas. A critical forum amongst people interested in seeing what could be learned about their work by taking new ideas seriously might form (Day 1984).

Such a critical forum might consider whether or not existing classroom routines are justified. Do classroom routines express the values which they are thought to? Are they justified? Not only is the learning process to be evaluated, but at issue is the role of the subject in the curriculum. In what sense does the subject matter matter? These are questions which emerge from the dialogue between innovative practices and existing routines – they are questions which innovative software leads teachers and developers to consider.

Forms of communication now exist for this potential to be realized, but they are not what now dominate professional development or research as we have seen. Dominant forms are aimed at the implementation of mandates – at compliance, as we saw; and research activity is used to engineer this compliance in the systems model we discussed above. Until the values and the problematics of classroom routines are taken more seriously, until the ideas and assumptions of innovations are made more transparent, and until illusions about innovations are punctured, it will be difficult for innovators and researchers to converse.

Dialogical research into these issues by teachers and outsiders is called for – an inquiry which is sensitive to their complexity. This means an approach to social science which attends to the meaning of the actions which it considers.

Such research takes seriously the context of action and so provides the basis for understanding the meaning of action in relation to the larger setting. This is why dialogical research as a methodological movement is important – it is based on a sound approach to the scientific study of social life. It is through such inquiry and the discourse it yields that the process of making new traditions will take place.

The process of change demands much of teachers. There are many temptations to pursue personal rewards rather than struggle with the difficult task of critical reflection. How are teachers to play a role in the change process itself, so that they can make sure that their experiences lead to professional development – to an increased capacity to pursue what is good for teaching? MacIntyre warns that:

Institutions are characteristically and necessarily concerned with what I have called external goods ... They are structured in terms of power and status, and they distribute money, power and status as rewards ... In this context the essential function of virtues is clear. Without them, without justice, courage and truthfulness practice could not resist the corrupting power of institutions.

(MacIntyre 1984: 194)

But what about the educational value of the innovation and the practices associated with it? What in this institutional process encourages critical thought about innovation? Very little. The reasons are complex. School system approved research models stultify critical thought (Schon 1983), career enhancement conflicts with educational values (Wilson 1962) and the technology is itself seductive (Jackson 1968). What can be done about this? How are these pitfalls to be avoided and good practice sustained? We must now consider these issues.

The moral basis of critical interpretation

What it takes to take teaching seriously

It takes courage to take one's teaching seriously. It also takes honesty and a sense of justice. These are virtues which teachers have to have if critical reflection is to occur and practice improve. How do we come to this conclusion? In this last section we shall consider the moral basis of critical reflection.

Teachers are being called to account – more so now than before because social problems are increasing. As these problems increase, schools are asked to provide solutions quickly and teachers are often criticized for contributing to the problems they are expected to help solve. How can schools give an accounting? Some, as we have seen, evoke science as a way of defending policy. They say that practice is based on the best social science available. Experts are called forward – usually from research institutes – to help the schools defend themselves. The mystique of science is used to defend the reputation of schools against criticism (Olson 1989a). Why won't this appeal to scientism work? Why can't schools rely on experts to defend what goes on there? The answer is simple – experts do not know the whole story; only a small part of it. Teachers know more.

Why do I say this? Is this not an empty slogan? No it is not, and for many reasons. Teachers speak on behalf of the educational interests of their students. They are well placed to defend the value of these goals – they stand up for the part of schooling that has education as a focus. Teachers know how to use the curriculum for educational purposes. They know what can be done, within the limits and limitations of policy, and they have practical knowledge about many of the essential problems of making curricula work. This knowledge has been gained from experience and reflection. The knowledge is shared. It is part of the oral culture of teaching (Reid 1990). Such knowledge is essential in the debate about schooling because grand visions for education derived from applied science are empty if they have no practical significance – indeed they are dangerous because they distract us from considering what is, in fact, being accomplished and what limits us from doing more. Put simply, teachers can subject visions to an analysis of their practical import, thereby becoming critics of promises that often are made which frequently serve the political needs of government but not necessarily the educational needs of students. Teachers embody moral values in their practice, they know how to use curricula and they have a basis for reflecting critically on practice. All of this is a potential. Whether or not it is realized is another matter. But it is a real potential.

In many places, however, this potential, unfortunately, is not being realized because teachers have little opportunity to reflect on the practices built on their professional life.

Most inquiry into education often is done as a way of engineering compliance to imposed policy – a basis for creating shaping forces outside the control of teachers (Franklin, 1990). Critical interpretation controlled by practitioners, on the other hand, can isolate boundaries of professional practice which should be expanded, reveal dysfunction and create solutions grounded in the moral basis of practice. What form this collaborative inquiry should take is an open question. Whatever form it takes, reflection on experience in order to reveal its moral basis ought to be at its heart.

Recovering the moral basis of practice is an exercise in historical reflection and reconstruction that has the power to shape the future. In this way curriculum reform and teacher reflection are intimately bound together. This view leaves considerable room for arguing about how teachers might become more self-critical, how severe the institutional constraints on critical reflection actually are and what might make education institutions more supportive of critical reflection.

Teachers ought to have a voice in the formulation of policy because their experience of enacting policy gives them essential know-how about realizing educational goals. Recovering the moral basis of this practice through reflection allows teachers to know their practice better, to criticize it and to represent what they know about practice in debates about schooling. Teachers teach better, directly because of increased consciousness about their values and how they affect practice, and indirectly through an increased capacity to argue for conditions which support better practice including improved curricula, better working conditions and increased commitment to education. How is this critical reflection to occur? Through the exercise of virtue.

While good practice can be explained in terms of virtues which sustain it, this is not a common way of looking at practice – to put it mildly. Normally practice is based on a technical rationale. Such technical bases for practice are flawed. Lacking a moral foundation, they are open to the abuse of power: 'we do what we do because, in the end, once past the appeal to science, powerful people say we ought to.' It is what the bureaucrats decide based on nothing more than the power they have that lies at the heart of technique.

We can base the practice of teaching on a moral foundation rather than a technical one. Let us consider how this can be done. The virtues of honesty, courage and justice are the bases of practice (MacIntyre 1984). These are conference points for explaining what practitioners do in their work, for identifying good practice, and sources of norms which ought to be cultivated:

> [Practice is] any coherent and complex form of socially established co-operative human activity through which goods internal to that form of activity are realized. Practice [provides] the arena in which the virtues are exhibited ... A practice involves standards of excellence and obedience to rules as well as achievement of goods.
>
> (MacIntyre 1984: 187, 190)

Teaching – a practice – is not aimed at production of something, but at developing and exercising the virtues of the group to which teacher and student belong – it is a moral enterprise, not a technical one. Thus it is misleading to talk of teaching as a craft. There may be 'crafty' elements, but it is essentially not a craft and not defined by technique.

In teaching, teachers strive to get students to look at the world in a critical way – a way whose qualities have to do with even-handedness, fair play and other standards which constitute the practice. These are standards teachers believe in – they try to get their charges to share their enthusiasm for them. Teachers work to improve their capacity to engender enthusiasm for critical and imaginative thought, amongst other things. Teachers are rewarded for their efforts to improve not only by seeing students better able to think well, but by being a teacher – by being engaged deeply in a morally worthwhile life.

A practice involves standards and obedience to rules as well as the achievement of the good things internal to the practice I have just mentioned. Although these standards change as they are tested in practice, they regulate contemporary practice: '[W]e cannot be initiated into a practice without accepting the authority of the best standards realized so far' (MacIntyre 1984: 190).

Achievement of the goals internal to a practice, MacIntyre says, requires virtue – virtue being 'an acquired human quality, the possession and exercise of which tends to enable us to achieve those goals which are internal to practice' (MacIntyre 1981: 191).

The concept of virtue thus is dependent on the nature of practice. Since practice is a social process in which some are better at it than others – better at meeting the highest standards, more knowledgeable about what ought to be done and how it ought to be done – initiates have to listen to their betters who urge them to take risks in the pursuit of excellence and who offer criticism to help them. What the initiate has to do requires virtue. One must be just – according respect where it is due; one must be courageous – take risks in trying to do what those who know better say we ought to do; one must be honest – listening carefully to what others say about one. Without these virtues, practices like teaching could not exist. These virtues make the practice possible and they make the practice what it is.

The practitioner needs to have three cardinal virtues: justice, honesty and courage. The person wanting to achieve the goals and meet the standards of the practice must, MacIntyre says:

> [recognize] what is due to whom; [take] self-endangering risks; [listen] carefully to what we are told about our own inadequacies . . . in other words, we have to accept as necessary components of any practice with internal good and standard of excellence the virtue of justice, courage and honesty.
>
> (MacIntyre 1984: 191)

Practices change over time – not just the techniques but the very goals of the practice. Those practising now are heirs to what has gone before – to the tradition which challenges people now to refine the standards and goals which contribute to the practice.

This account of the nature of a practice has important implications for how we construe teacher education – especially in-service education. Clearly, we have to accord importance to outstanding practitioners – master teachers – they have much to teach us. We also have to ensure that the history of the practice is well written. We must encourage teachers to speak the truth when the goals of the institution conflict with those of the practice – when what the 'system' wants is against what is good for the practice of teaching.

Those of us who practice do not always achieve the good the practice sets out to achieve, for it is hard to avoid being 'seduced' by good external to the practice, as we saw here and see in our professional lives. Thus the diagnosis of dysfunction is a crucial task for the student of practice – insider or outsider because it is important to know where the perils lie, what causes practice to 'go off the rails'. The shared commitment to the internal good things of the practice of teaching makes it worthwhile to consider the collective health of the community of practitioners, and legitimates taking each other's practice seriously – that is, critically. It is what allows me *not* to feel that I am scourging Ms Abt, but instead seeking a common purpose in the face of common pitfalls to good practice.

Teachers work in conflicted situations because they work in institutions. Those very conflicts, the passions they arouse and the threats they entail for teaching are how the goals and standards of practice become better understood. Threat teaches us what we value. Such threats to practice ought to form major topics for reflection – for teacher education.

Given that teaching is a moral enterprise, critical appraisal of new forms of practice and of the institutionalization of change itself are an essential part of reflection and of inquiry. While all educators are involved in these processes, major responsibility for worthwhile educational practice in schools falls to teachers who must maintain an uneasy relationship with school bureaucracies. These offer seductive new technologies as career enhancement and other goods but do not encourage reflection on the moral basis of practice (Olson 1989b). It takes virtue to critically reflect on practice.

Practices take place within institutions – often bureaucratic institutions. Their institutions face outward to the larger society and pursue goals external to practice – goals to do with money, fame, prestige, power. A tension exists between these external goals and those which constitute the practice itself.

Teachers work in school systems – institutions largely concerned about external goals. Who then speaks for the goals of teaching? Who understands the significance of virtue as a basis for practice? Teachers understand these things. Outstanding practice ought to be studied and its documents made into the kind of history which would serve the building of a tradition reflecting the moral basis of practice.

This implies that excellent teachers will have to be taken much more seriously than before because of what they can tell us about achieving the goals of teaching and about the tradition they represent. It also implies that the search for the justification of practice in technique is a false path. Excellence is dependent on virtue foremostly – only on technique in a subsidiary way. We need to ask how virtue can be acquired by practitioners so they might begin to profit from the tradition, from other colleagues, from students and from their own reflected-upon experience.

Teachers work in an essentially conflicted situation about which, as MacIntyre (1984) suggests, we ought not to ask what end or purposes does [it] serve, but rather of *what* conflict is it the scene? He says, 'it is through conflict and sometimes only through conflict that we learn what our ends and purposes are'.

This is the reason why it is valuable to reflect on practice in relation to its institutional setting and why teachers must become alert to the ways in which the institutions of schooling can undermine their own practice. Thinking critically about those conflicts is a way to improve practice itself and build valid institutions in which practice can improve. Reflecting on practice aids in developing good schools through ethically justified innovation. This is the link between interpretation and the improvement of education that ought to be made.

References

Argyris, C. and Schon, D. (1974). *Theory in Practice: Increasing Professional Effective-ness*. San Francisco: Jossey Bass.

Bannister, D. and Mair, J. M. (1968). *The Evaluation of Personal Constructs*. London: Academic Press.

Benner, P. (1984). *From Novice to Expert*. Menlo Park: Addison Wesley.

Berliner, D. (1989). 'The place of process-product research in developing the agenda for research on teacher thinking'. In J. Lowyck and C. Clark (eds), *Teacher Thinking and Professional Action*. Louvain: Louvain University Press.

Berliner, D. and Carter, K. (1989). 'Differences in processing classroom information by expert and novice teachers'. In J. Lowyck and C. Clark (eds), *Teacher Thinking and Professional Action*. Louvain: Louvain University Press.

Brine, J. (1983). *The Microcomputer Threat to Classroom Order*. Paper presented at the annual CSSE conference. Vancouver, Canada, June.

Broome, R. (1989). 'The "collective student" as the cognitive reference point of teachers' thinking about their students in the classroom'. In J. Lowyck and C. Clark (eds), *Teacher Thinking and Professional Action*. Louvain: Louvain University Press.

Buchman, M. (1987). 'Teaching knowledge: The lights that teachers live by'. In A. Stromnes and N. Sovik (eds), *Teachers Thinking*. Trondheim: Tapir Press.

Carlgren, I. (1989). 'School-centered innovations and teacher rationality'. In J. Lowyck and C. Clark (eds), *Teacher Thinking and Professional Action*. Louvain: Louvain University Press.

Collingwood, R. G. (1946). *The Idea of History*. Oxford: Oxford University Press.

Connelly, F. M. (1972). 'The functions of curriculum development', *Interchange* **3**: 161–77.

Day, C. (1984). 'Teachers' thinking: an action research perspective'. In R. Halks and J. Olson (eds), *Teacher Thinking*. Lisse: Swets and Zeitlinger.

Doyle, W. and Ponder, G. A. (1977). 'The practicality ethic in teacher decision-making', *Interchange* **8**: 1–12.

Dray, W. (1957). *Laws and Explanation in History*. Oxford: Oxford University Press.

Dreeben, R. (1970). *The Nature of Teaching: Schools and the Work of Teachers*. Glenview: Scott, Forsman.

Dreyfus, H. and Dreyfus, S. (1986). *Mind over Machine*. New York: Free Press.

Fenstermacher, G. D. (1978). 'A philosophical consideration of recent research on teacher effectiveness', *Review of Research in Education* 6: 157–85.

Franklin, U. (1990). *The Real World of Technology*. Toronto: CBC Enterprises.

Fransella, F. (1988). 'PCT: Still radical thirty years on?' In F. Fransella and L. Thomas (eds), *Experimenting with Personal Construct Psychology*. New York: Routledge & Kegan Paul.

Freire, P. (1973). *Education for Critical Consciousness*. New York: Seabury Press.

Fussell, P. (1980). *Abroad*. Oxford: Oxford University Press.

Gagné, R. M. (1965). *The Conditions of Learning*. New York: Holt, Rinehart & Winston.

Geertz, C. (1973). *The Interpretation of Cultures*. New York: Basic Books.

Gudmundsdottir, S. and Schulman, L. (1989). 'Pedagogical knowledge in social studies'. In J. Lowyck and C. Clark (eds), *Teacher Thinking and Professional Action*. Louvain: Louvain University Press.

Harre, R. (1979). *Social Being*. Oxford: Oxford University Press.

Hall, G. and Loucks, S. (1977). 'A developmental model to determine whether treatment is actually implemented', *American Education Research Journal* 14: 263–76.

House, E. R. (1974). *The Politics of Curriculum Innovation*. Berkeley: McCutchan.

Hudson, L. (1975). *The Psychology of Human Experience*. New York: Anchor Books.

Jackson, P. (1968). *The Teacher and the Machine*. Pittsburgh: Pittsburgh University Press.

Jordell, K. (1987). 'Teachers as reflective practitioners'. In A. Stromnes and N. Sovik (eds), *Teachers Thinking*. Trondheim: Tapir Press.

Kelly, G. (1955). *The Psychology of Personal Constructs*. New York: Norton.

Leinhardt, G. (1986). 'Math lessons: a contrast of novice and expert competence'. In J. Lowyck (ed.), *Teacher Thinking and Professional Action*. Proceedings of the third ISATT conference. Leuven: ISATT.

Lortie, D. (1973). 'Observations on teaching as work'. In R. M. Travers (ed.), *Second Handbook of Research on Teaching*. Chicago: Rand McNally.

Lortie, D. (1975). *Schoolteacher*. Chicago: University of Chicago Press.

MacIntyre, A. (1984). *After Virtue*. Notre Dame: Notre Dame University Press.

Mancuso, J. and Eimer, B. (1982). 'A constructivist view of reprimand in the classroom', *Interchange* 13: 39–46.

Meyer, J. W. (1980). 'Levels of the educational system and schooling effects'. In C. E. Bidwell and D. M. Windham (eds), *The Analysis of Educational Productivity*, No. 1, 2, *Issues in Microanalysis*. Cambridge, Mass.: Ballinger.

Mischel, T. (1964). 'Personal constructs, rules and the logic of clinical activity', *Psychological Review* 71: 180–92.

National Science Foundation (1978). *Case Studies in Science Education*. Urbana-Champaign: University of Illinois.

Olson, J. (1980). 'Teacher constructs and curriculum change', *Journal of Curriculum Studies* 7: 1–11.

Olson, J. (1981). 'Teacher influence in the classroom: A context for understanding curriculum change', *Instructional Science* 10: 259–75.

Olson, J. (1982). 'Classroom knowledge and curriculum change'. In J. Olson (ed.), *Innovation in the Science Curriculum*. London: Croom Helm.

Olson, J. (1988). *Schoolworlds/Microworlds: Computers and the Culture of the School*. Oxford: Pergamon.

Olson, J. (1989a). 'The persistence of technical rationality'. In G. Milburn *et al.* (eds), *Re-interpreting Curriculum Research: Images and Arguments*. Lewes: Falmer Press.

Olson, J. (1989b). 'Surviving innovation: reflection on the pitfalls of practice', *Journal of Curriculum Studies* 21: 503–8.

Olson, J. and Eaton, S. (1986). *Case Studies of Microcomputers in the Classrooms*. Toronto: Queen's Printer.

Olson, J. and Eaton, S. (1987). 'Curriculum changes and the classroom order'. In J. Calderhead (ed.), *Exploring Teachers' Thinking*. London: Cassell.

Perrow, C. (1965). 'Hospitals: Technology, structure and goals'. In J. March (ed.), *Handbook of Organizations*. Chicago: Rand McNally.

Peters, R. S. and White, J. P. (1973). 'The philosopher's contribution to educational research'. In W. Taylor (ed.), *Research Perspectives in Education*. London: Routledge & Kegan Paul.

Polanyi, M. (1958). *The Study of Man*. Chicago: University Press.

Pope, M. (1978). 'Monitoring and reflecting in teacher training'. In F. Fransella (ed.), *Personal Construct Psychology*. London: Academic Press.

Reid, W. A. (1978). *Thinking About the Curriculum*. London: Routledge & Kegan Paul.

Reid, W. A. (1979). 'Making the problem fit the method: A review of the "Banbury Enquiry" ', *Journal of Curriculum Studies* 11: 167–73.

Reid, W. A. (1990). *Literacy, Orality, and the Functions of Curriculum*. Unpublished.

Ryle, G. (1949). *The Concept of Mind*. London: Hutchinson.

Schon, D. (1983). *The Reflective Practitioner*. New York: Basic Books.

Scheingold, K. (1981). *Issues Related to the Implementation of Computer Technology in Schools*. New York: Bank Street College.

Shulman, L. (1987). 'Knowledge and teaching: Foundation for the new reform', *Harvard Educational Review* 57: 1–22.

Sieber, S. D. (1972). 'Images of the practitioner and strategies of educational change', *Sociology of Education* 45: 358–62.

Vickers, G. (1970). *Freedom in a Rocking Boat*. London: Penguin.

Weick, K. (1976). 'Educational organizations as loosely coupled systems', *Administrative Science Quarterly* 21: 1–19.

Westbury, I. (1973). 'Conventional classrooms, "Open" classrooms and the technology of teachers', *Journal of Curriculum Studies* 5: 99–121.

Wilson, B. (1962). 'The teacher's role: A sociological analysis', *British Journal of Sociology* 13: 22.

Wilson, J. (1979). *Fantasy and Commonsense in Education*. New York: John Wiley.

Index